Blackden

Duncan McLean was born in Aberdeenshire
in 1964 and now lives in Orkney. His first book,
Bucket of Tongues, won a Somerset Maugham
award in 1993. His play, *Julie Allardyce*,
is published by Methuen, and his latest novel
is *Bunker Man*.

Duncan McLean

BLACKDEN

Minerva

A Minerva Paperback
BLACKDEN

First published in Great Britain 1994
by Martin Secker & Warburg Limited
This Minerva edition published 1995
by Mandarin Paperbacks
an imprint of Reed Consumer Books Ltd
Michelin House, 81 Fulham Road, London SW3 6RB
and Auckland, Melbourne, Singapore and Toronto

A CIP catalogue record for this title
is available from the British Library
ISBN 0 7493 9634 2

The author thanks the Scottish Arts Council
for a bursary which helped him during
the writing of this book.

Printed and bound in Great Britain
by Cox & Wyman Ltd, Reading, Berkshire

for
Ronald and Margaret Harper
and
David and Alice Stevenson

Friday

The track down from Goodman's Croft was rutted with mud, kirned up into a furrow of dried dubs and sharn in the middle, with more muck flung onto the long grass and tangled whins that lined it all the way to its junction with the denside road. For twenty years the only thing to come up the half-mile hill had been Dod of Goodman's old grey Fordson, a bogey of neeps for the beasts bouncing along behind, Dod himself perched on top, bony arse padded from the iron seat by a thickfolded tattie-sack. But this morning the Murray Marts van had won through the dirt and shite and parked at the top of the brae. It'd stayed there all day till a few minutes before, when it rattled off downhill again.

Now the van was pausing near the foot of the track, and I was lining up the front wheel of my bike in one of its tyre-tracks, hoping to get a half-smooth run down to the road. I slung my leg over the crossbar, and the van turned right and motored away along the road into the depths of the wood that covered the den. As I pushed off and jolted down the first stretch of the track I could see the steady red of its tail-lights and the occasional sweep of its main-beamers cutting through the trees, but inside half a minute it was right into the denseness of the woods and I'd lost it.

I looked back to the track. The bike was juttering and my bones with it as the wheels ran over rocks and holes and skites of muddy grass. I kept my hands on the cool metal brake-levers to check my speed, and balanced my weight on the pedals, hovering just off the saddle, but there was no use: it was a rough ride down and that was all the story.

What made it worse was the darkness inbetween the trackside dykes and the high straggly bushes. The sky above was mostly clear, except for some long streaks of browny clouds lying across the howe like muck shot out of a spreader, but the woods along the den were black ahead, and the chinks in the dykes and the neuks round the roots of the whins were black as well, and they sucked the light out of the air leaving only shadows across the way, till my eyes were straining to see where I was heading. And all I could hear was the clattering bike, the rusty chain creaking, chuckies skittering out from under my tyres.

At last I was down the worst of the brae, and the track flattened out, less worn and rutted here by channels and pirls of rainflow, less broken up by the hooves of Dod's beasts cloitering to get a grip on the steepness of the slope on their way from park to byre. I eased off the brakes and picked up some speed, feeling for the first time the coldness of the early night air as I cut through it – steering on the level straight and easy, fingers loose on the rubber grips, backside resting on the saddle. My body relaxed forward into a curve, tired after the work of the day. And now I was out of the tunnel of whins too, coasting along in the open for a spell before I'd be back into the darkness of the woods ahead.

I raised my head as I rode, looked up at the stars pricking out all over the darkening sky, felt the cold air pressing against my throat. And as I came towards the end of the track I could feel dampness, a cool clammy dampness rising from the pools and bogs of the den, the smell of mouldering leaves and bracken and other dead growth seeping up with it. Down in the wet cleft of the den the winter rot was already setting in, the willows and birks stripped bare, the giant bracken and hogweed, half-strangled by an undergrowth of brambles all summer, grey and dead now and sinking down on top of the briers to rot and fume.

Reaching the junction, I skidded round in a half-circle to stop. I wanted to rest a second to settle my jarred bones back into their joints before setting off along the road to the village at the head of the den. My backside was still aching, so I eased forward off the saddle and propped my elbows on the handlebars, feet flat on the ground. A piece of board with a Murray Marts poster tacked on it had been hung from the signpost at the end of the track, the red marker lettering saying: ROUP – ALL GOOD'S AND GEAR, Saturday 14th November, 10 a.m. – viewing from 9.

I'd been told to get there two hours before the selling started so I could finish getting the lots all laid out and numbered and tables set up ready for Mrs Murray to serve the teas and pieces on. Me and her and her man Bill had been trying to do it all in a oner today, but the shortness of the notice for the whole sale meant we didn't realise what a heap of stuff there was to be sorted. Also, Bill Murray had had to shoot off smart to canvass a couple Donsiders about business for next week's cattle mart. This gave me an early start in the morning, but a sharp finish now and a free evening ahead.

It was Friday night and the lights were coming on at the Auld Mill Inn. I pushed off and cranked full steam for Blackden.

*

I arrived in the village just as the evening bus from Aberdeen was pulling in at the shelter, and coasted to a stop to see who'd be getting off. A couple kids in uniform: the vet's lads back from their private school. Half a dozen low-ranking commuters returning from their jobs in banks and shops and offices. Crabbit Miss McAndrew who used to run the post office: she set off towards the council houses, walking at a running pace as usual, the weight of three laden carrier bags in each hand making her lurch from side to side as she went, till she looked in danger of toppling right over and rolling into the gutter, where she'd lie all night, legs still whirring away in mid-air.

Last off the bus was Dek Duguid, who I've kent since primary school. I waited till the bus drew out of the square then shouted on him.

Hey man, Dek!

Aye, Paddy. He nodded and looked both ways along the silent street before crossing to where I was sitting. Still riding this old cunt of a bike? he said as he approached, and kicked at my front spokes with the toe of his trainer.

Still riding that old cunt of a bus?

Pff! He shrugged, started scuffing his heel into a patch of crumbling tarmac. Looks like I won't be getting the bastard much longer if I don't start pulling my finger out at the old fucking college.

What! Three months in, you bastard, and they're giving you the boot?

He shrugged again, looked down. My spokes had printed a web of greasy black lines on his white toecap. Well, maybe, just . . .

And you were so keen to get there and that! Nights of swotting for the resits! What's up with you, man?

Dek shook his head. There's a lot of distractions, ken? It's hard

4

to mind you're there to learn about fucking trees sometimes. Maybe you had the right idea, Paddy: straight into the fucking job, bit of siller in your pocket and that.

Not much though, Dek, not what you'd call. . .

Christ, I might as well be at school sometimes! Do this, do that. . . Fucking homework: disaster!

I looked away down the street. The last of the folk off the bus had disappeared and the whole of the square and the streets off it were empty, no cars parked outside the Auld Mill even. Teatime: the place was dead.

Fuck, that's atrocious, I said.

Dek hadn't raised his head. Ken what they had us doing theday? Ancient history. The prehistoric woodlands of Caledonia. What's that got to do with fuck all?

Well. . .I don't know. But it'll be good when you finish and that, eh? I mean the pay with the Forestry, you with your degree and everything.

It's all so miles off though, Paddy. I'm in a limbo, hanging in limbo just! Give me a chainsaw now and I'll cut their bastarding trees down, I don't need a college degree to do that!

I pushed off on the bike and started to cycle slowly round the square. Well, I shouted in Dek's direction, The great thing is you'll save a lot of energy with your education. Instead of sawing the trees down, you can just argue with the buggers, *persuade* them to lie down for you.

Ach. . .you don't understand, Paddy, it's not funny. He stopped watching me arsing around and walked off towards his street, piecebag of books dragging along the pavement at his heels. I stood up on the pedals and nipped alongby him.

Here, never mind fucking trees, Dek! Maybe you could persuade some woman to lie down for you!

Shut up, he said, and swung his bag of books in my direction. You're a pain in the butt with your fucking wisecracks all the time.

Butt! I cried, What's a butt? He didn't reply. I biked on ahead a wee bit, then swung the old crate round in a skid to block his path. Can I help it if I'm a cheery soul?

Can I help it if I give you a smack on the chin? he said, stepping around my back wheel.

I shoved off again. Does the college give you lessons in that andall then? I said. Cause you were piss-poor at fighting last I saw of it.

You learn a lot of things at the college, he said.

Here, Dek. Mind at New Year when you blootered that Kemnay loon over the skull with your mope helmet? Skill! They couldn't teach you that for sure.

Dek was grinning, remembering. Christ aye, Paddy: that was a brilliant laugh.

Aye, I saw the guy giggling as they carried him away. . .

Oi, cried Dek, stopping in the middle of the road so I just about collided with him. Who're you to slag off my fighting anyhow? Least I do lash out from time to time!

I stopped the bike and looked at him. You saying I don't lash out?

Course I'm saying you don't lash out, you cunt! He laughed, started walking again. What a nerve, he said as he passed me.

Well, I'm not going to hit just anybody, I said. I mean they'd have to really deserve it, ken.

Bollocks! You're found out. He laughed some more, striding away up the street.

I biked towards him in a wavering curve across the road. What's so funny?

You! Trying to be all fucking logical about putting the boot in. It doesn't work like that: if you thought about it logically you wouldn't fucking do it at all.

We turned into Dek's street, and my spine jarred as the bike ran over a hole in the road.

That's your problem, Paddy, he went on. Trying to be logical all the time. Fuck it! Go with the flow!

I do! I do go with the flow! Christ, I'm always trying to go with the flow. . . I leant over the handlebars and heaved away at the thing for a few seconds, till I'd gone right past Dek's house. My face was burning and my heart battering. I slowed and looked back. Dek had turned up his garden path and was trudging along between the skeletons of his father's roses, hands stuck in his pockets, eyes down. I wheeled the crate round once more and freewheeled back down the incline. He didn't look up, but I shouted as I passed, See you in the Mill thenight, then we'll go along to the stovie dance, eh? I'll show you going with the flow man!

He didn't answer, or I didn't hear him if he did. All that came was the bang of the front door shutting behind him. I laid into the pedals and dreeled back through the village, heading for home.

I had my head down over the handlebars, so I didn't notice the car was gone till I rounded the last bend in the track and came to a stop at the side of the house. It was a cold night up there on the hill, but sweat was dripping off me, and I had to shake my head like a dog to fling it out of my stinging eyes. I looked around till I got my breath back; there were no lights on, no smoke in the lum, and the Lada was gone from the lean-to port against the shed. I got off the bike and wheeled it through the chuckies on the turning-circle, then leant it against the wall of chopped logs piled at the gable-end of the house. I took my piece-box out of the basket over the front wheel and walked, whistling a bit of nothing, to the door. It was locked. Nobody had ever bothered to give me a key of my own, but most of the time it didn't matter. In fact it didn't matter now either; under a fallen slate on the sill of the window next to the door was a spare. I got it out, opened the door, slipped the key back into its hiding place, and walked in.

The first thing I saw in the kitchen was a great screed of a note in the middle of the table. I took a kind of swerving step towards it, just close enough to see that it didn't have big letters saying GET OUT NOW, THE HOUSE IS GOING TO EXPLODE, then went on along to the lavvy.

I pished and washed. My ma's a great one for notes. It started a couple year ago, when she was having difficulties speaking without bursting out greeting. Writing seemed to be easier for her. One morning around that time, the end of the summer holidays, I came down for breakfast to find a note in my bowl. It said:

Patrick – Remember you start
back at the school today. Up sharp
and out of here by 8. M.

I laughed over this, then I said to her as I was pouring out my cornflakes – cause she was right there at the table, she wasn't away to work or anything – I said, Ma, what's the point of you leaving me a note saying to get up early? You should've given me a shout. If I hadn't got up early I'd be late already! She shrugged and took a slurp of her tea. Sorry, she said. Sorry? I said, Don't be daft,

8

there's nothing to be. . . It's funny, that's what it is, Ma, funny! I took another mouthful of cornflakes and a trickle of milk escaped from the corner of my mouth as I laughed. Honest, Ma, if the house was on fire and I was in my bed, I bet you wouldn't wake me up, I bet you'd just leave a note stuck to the bedroom door:

<u>Patrick</u> – Run for your life,
we're all going to die. <u>M</u>

Hmm, she went, getting up from the table. Maybe I should write that up anyway, even without the fire. And she tiptoed upstairs with a cup of tea for my da.

Up in my bedroom, I put on some new clothes, ran the electric shaver over a couple places on my face, then slapped on some aftershave. I have this theory that you have to really fucking belt the stuff onto your face, not just pat it on gently. If you give it a good whack then the smell of the stuff gets pushed right into your pores, right under your skin, and so takes longer to wear off. I'm determined to get my money's worth.

Cheeks tingling from the slaps, I headed downstairs, the memory seeping into my brain that the aftershave was actually a present from my gran and granda last christmas, so it wasn't my money I was getting the worth of, but the old folks. All the more reason. One day, five years after me getting them first, my granda noticed that my face was all broken out in plooks. In fact there were so many of the bastards that they were just about all joined up, my whole face was one big plook more or less. I was scared to squeeze them, in case my whole head came spurting out and my skull caved in completely. You should try some of that extra strong Old Spice, my granda said. The reek of that'll burn them off in no time. I didn't believe him to begin with, but that

9

christmas a bottle of the stuff turned up under the tree and I slapped it on and. . .it worked.

<u>Patrick</u> – That's me off then. (4 o'clock.)
   I'll be leaving Ed early on Sun, so will see
      you when I get back. The roads should be
         quiet. If anything comes up, Helen's number
            is in the book. Have a good weekend. <u>M</u>.
<u>P.S.</u> Janice next door is doing it tomorrow but can't tonight,
   so could you? Yankee doodle pie in the fridge, stick it in the
      oven 20 min 200 – stay till your granda's taken it out,
         otherwise he'll likely forget and burn it to a crisp, and
            crisps get stuck beneath his plate. <u>M</u>.

<u>M</u> for Ma and also for Moira. I went to the fridge. There was a casserole with a tinfoil lid that would be the grub for the old folks. There was also a bowl with cooked mince set in it, white fat formed on the surface in all the pits and crannies, like ice fastened round crumbly dark lumps of soil in a ploughed park. Delicious. I took the mince and marge out and got a couple slices of bread from the bin marked READ. My sister whited out the first letter just before she first went away to college, after getting food-poisoning off an out-of-date packet of potato scones. The idea was that the message on the bin would remind her to check the labels before stuffing anything in her mouth in future. I suggested writing on something clearer, like BEWARE THE SKITTERS! but Helen told me this just wasn't funny, and Ma backed her up. I shouldn't've been surprised: Ma was always siding with her, even then.

Waiting for the kettle to boil, I spread the bread, piled on the mince, then squidged the whole thing together between my palms and started eating. Excellent grub. Which is a shame, cause I've been thinking recently about stopping eating meat, even borderline cases like Butcher Wolfe's mince. I have this theory that you should only eat an animal if you've slaughted it yourself in fair and equal combat and are willing to take it home, cut it up and cook it with your own fair hands. And wear the shrunken head of the thing round your neck for luck afterwards like the cannibals do.

By the time the water was boiled, I'd finished my sandwich, so I made another one to go with my coffee: jam this time. I took the cup and sandwich over to the table and sat there eating and drinking, trying to work out which tasted better: a mouthful of half-chewed bread having coffee sluiced in after it, or a mouthful of coffee having dauds of bread dropped in to float and gradually soak it up, or maybe the mouth being completely emptied by swallowing one thing before introducing the other at all. The bastard of it was, none of these seemed to be better than the others. Typical. You get presented with what looks like a great choice between a wide range of options, then when you get to the bottom of it the whole lot are all the fucking same: plain old sandwich and coffee, however much you try and kid yourself.

The jam was definitely good though, extremely excellent: bramble jam, made by my gran. As I ate, letting seeds stick inbetween my teeth quite happily – knowing I'd be able to pick them out with my tongue later and get that wee burst of taste as I nipped them open – I was minded on the night a couple weeks before, when my ma had first taken this particular jar of jam out of the cupboard and put it on the teatable. I'd been sitting there, eating my chips, when I noticed her kind of frozen, staring at the slip of paper sellotaped to the lid. What's up, Ma? I said.

I've just noticed the date of this, she said. It's probably the last jar of jam your gran'll ever make.

Oh no. Is that the last of hers? The shop-bought stuff doesn't taste half so good!

Oh Patrick. . . She let go of the jar and it fell onto the table from about ten cm. up, then rolled over against my plate. I looked up at her in amazement, then looked again, more amazed: she was greeting.

Ma. . .eh. . .what's the matter? She shook her head, took a hankie out from her sleeve and began mopping up around her eyes. Look, I said, The bought stuff's not that bad! She turned away from me, went over to the cooker and started stirring the stock-bone round and round in the broth. The bone clunked on the metal, and she grat. Ma, I said, You'll make the soup salty.

One of her sobs was almost a laugh.

It was embarrassing. I looked down at my chips, then back at her. I didn't know what to say. I'd never known what to say, but in the past it didn't usually matter much. Now I had to say something: there was nobody else around to do it.

Alright, so Gran's maybe no fit to be boiling jam and jelly any more. I paused, she sniffed, I went on. But you ken what like Granda is. Come the season he'll be out on his bike, away all the banks and braes, filling his carrier bags with rasps and brambles. No sign of him slowing up! He kens all the best places: redcurrants, gooseberries, blaeberries. . .

Och. . . She sighed loudly, staring into the soup pot still. That makes it worse, she said. Your granda collecting pounds of fruit and Gran stuck in her bed. It'll all just rot away. It's a waste, a terrible waste.

It won't rot! Get it up here, we'll make the jam!

Oh Patrick, when have I the time to make jam these days? Inbetween the job and everything.

Alright, alright, I'll make it. You tell me how, show me the cookbook even, and I'll make the jam. It'd be good, I'd like to do it!

It's not out of a cookbook, she said.

Shortly after, she went down to see them with their evening meal. She did this when nobody else had volunteered. She did it most days, except once in a blue moon when a neighbour did. The idea was that they should get something hot once a day at least; my gran couldn't get near her kitchen now, and the only thing my granda could make was porridge.

By the time she left for the village she'd cheered up a bit, and she clapped me on the shoulder as she passed to go out to the car. Me and her get on fine, I'd say we get on well, even though she prefers Helen really. The way we get on well is this: she never interferes with anything that's important to me, only stupid wee things like getting to work on time or talking to the old folks, which I'd do anyway. Anything that's important to me she never touches on. In fact she has no idea what's important to me, that's how she doesn't interfere with it; if she did know, probably she would. But I keep her out by keeping these important things buried deep down; I never let her get a glisk of them.

I'd finished eating long syne, and was sitting at the table, staring at nothing. I became aware that my cock was hard, hard as a stick of Edinburgh rock. I put my hand down and rubbed my fist up and down against it through the denim of my jeans. Spunk would be running the length of it like lettering through Edinburgh rock.

I stopped. I'd washed, I was just away out, tonight might even be the night I'd need a full cockful. Imagine the

13

humiliation of pulling yourself out of some lassie and her looking down at the frenchie and going, Christ, what's that, cuckoo spit?

I stood up, eased my breeks down between my legs a bit, and walked around the room. No use. Jesus, what had I been thinking about? Nothing at all! Fucking jam recipies! Sex hadn't come into it!

Cold shower time.

I went over to the sink, took the plastic basin out, then turned on the cold tap and let it flow till it was icy. I opened the spaver, eased down the front of my ys, then leant forward on my tiptoes and pointed my stiff cock under the jet of water. Fuck! Cold! Immediately the thing began to shrivel. I wiggled it around a bit, watching it shrink away, then looked up as something caught my eye. A grinning face was looking in the window at me, directly above the sink.

It was my auntie Heather. She waved, I raised one hand to wave back, and jammed the other one down into the sink in front of my open flies. I could feel my face bursting out in a hot red beamer. Heather disappeared in the direction of the door, and I quickly pushed my cock away, still dripping wet, pulled the front of my ys out over it and yanked up my zip.

Hellooo! The kitchen door opened, and Heather stuck the top half of her body round it, a grin on her face.

I turned back to the sink immediately, snatched up the squeezy bottle and squirted a jet of green liquid into the sink. It frothed up under the spray from the tap. I chanced a look round. Hello Heather, come in!

But she already had come in, and was looking at me and the

14

basin with a frown on her face. You'd be better with the plug in, she said.

Oh aye! Hih! I grabbed the chain from where it was twisted round the tap. The plug swung back and cracked me on the knuckles, making me jerk my hand away, jerk it under the full force of the cold tap. Water sprayed up all over me and the draining board and the window, and I could hear it spattering on the lino. I finally got the plug fitted into its hole, Heather laughing away behind me, then stared at the water gushing into the sink. She said something, but the sound of the water covered it up. I shut the tap off and turned to her. What?

She had sat down at the table and was rummaging around in her bag. I was just saying, she said, Would you not be better off with hot water? She pulled out a packet of B&H and a lighter, then looked up at me.

I was just going to, I said. You should always put the cold in first, did you not ken? I mean what if a toddler came along and tumbled into a sinkful of scalding water? It wouldn't do him any good if you put the cold in five minutes later, would it?

Patrick, there's no wee kids in this house.

I ken, I ken, but, eh. . .it's the principle. I mean I might've tripped myself and gone in head first, or. . .anything!

She looked at me. I worry about you sometimes, boy.

No need to worry, Heather, I'm dead safety conscious. As you can see. I reached behind me and put the other tap on. Ow! I made on I'd burnt my hand in the stream of hot water.

She smiled, tapped a cigarette on the tabletop and raised it to her lips. Then she lowered it again. I take it your mother is out?

Aye.

She nodded, flicked her lighter, lit the fag, and inhaled. I saw the car was gone when I came up, so I thought she was probably away somewhere. She breathed out a lungful of smoke. I was just going to go away again, but I thought I'd keek in the window in case anybody else was at home. And I fair got a surprise when I saw you.

Eh. . .I was washing the dishes.

Aye, so I saw. That was what surprised me: a man doing the housework! The window was that dirty I couldn't make out it was you really. Still, it would've been more of a surprise if it had been any other man, I suppose.

I turned back to the sink, put off the hot tap.

I mean. . . I'm sorry, Paddy. I meant, if your mother had got some new good-looking guy in her life. And in her kitchen.

I collected my plate and mug from the table, and the knife and mincebowl from beside the kettle, and dumped them in the sink. I stuck my hands in amongst them and swirled the water about. Aye, no bother, Heather. I kent you were meaning that. You wouldn't make jokes.

And listen, Paddy: I ken your mother doesn't like me smoking, but do you mind? I'll easy put it out.

I shrugged, my hands in the warm water up to the wrists, just where you'd slice a razor across them. It's your cancer, I said, You feed it how you like.

Silence. Then, I'm sorry, she said again.

I clattered the dishes around in the sink, rubbed at them with my fingers, then lifted them onto the rack at the side to dry.

I am intending to give up, she said, But it's hard. You come to depend on them, you know. There'd be no point giving them up if you were to get an ulcer from the nerves or get fat from eating chocolate instead. I mean it's to do with mental health as well as physical health.

I pulled out the plug and watched the grey water circle down

16

the drain, dirty froth and particles of mince and gravy carried away in it. It gurgled like a choking man as the last swirl went down. I reached for a teatowel hanging on the cupboard door and dried my hands.

At least if you're alive you're able to worry and eat, I said. It doesn't do any good having perfect mental health if you're dead from poisoned lungs. I looked over; Heather was stubbing out her fag, forehead puckered. Ach Jesus! Heather, I don't mean to hassle you, it's just. . .you shouldn't get me started on the subject, that's all. If I don't speak about it it's okay, cause then I don't think about it. Sorry.

No, no. I'm sorry. The cigarette was dead, but she kept on stubbing at it.

God, will you listen to us. I went and sat down opposite her. Sorry sorry sorry. . . It's pathetic! There's too much sorriness in the world, not enough, not enough. . .something.

Coffee, she said quietly, after a few seconds.

Aye, coffee, that's it: there's not enough coffee in the world! And ken this, the idea's just come into my head, would you like one?

She looked up, beginning to smile. A coffee? Mm, aye, that would be grand. I mean I'm not staying or anything, but a coffee, aye.

I went to get up from the table, but she beat me to it, putting her hand on my shoulder for a second as she passed. I'll get it, she said. Least I can do.

She filled the kettle up at the sink, then plugged it back in and wandered off around the kitchen, looking at the photos on the walls: my da and ma together, my sister, my ma and Heather and their brother Angus, one of Angus by himself in his orange survival suit, black sea and grey sky behind him. Heather stopped at the calendar, and bent over to peer at the scribbled words and circle around this weekend's dates.

What's this? Ed Hel squiggle. . .

I glanced down at my ma's note, still on the table. It means she's gone to Edinburgh to see Helen. I suppose she must've told me, but. . .

And how's she getting on these days? Still liking it?

I shrugged. No idea. Do you think I talk to her or something? Patrick!

Nah, ask my ma when she gets back. She'll have all the latest news. I'd just be guessing. God, I've enough of a job trying to remember what I'm doing, never mind keeping track of my brainy sister too.

Psh. She moved on and looked out the window, though with it being more or less completely dark outside, she might well have been spying on me in the reflection. You could've gone too, she said after a moment. We need more Scottish folk at Scottish unis and colleges.

Aye, but not more stupid folk.

Patrick, don't speak rubbish!

Wait! I jumped up from the table, a finger held in the air, and went over to the cooker. I studied the digital clock by the controls. Will you look at that, I said. Quarter to seven!

Have you not got a watch?

What? Aye. But you might not've believed me. I mean you might've thought I was just making it up when I said it was late if I just glanced at my watch then stowed it away again. I mean I might've been lying about it for some secret motive. Whereas if I actually show you it on the cooker, if I actually point out the trusty old digits on the electric clock, well, then you can't doubt, then you have to believe me.

You're mad boy! What on earth secret motive could you possibly have?

Hih, well, I do have one actually: I'm supposed to be making tea for my gran and granda Hunter thenight.

Ach, you should've said.

I went over to the fridge.

God, first you're washing the dishes, now you're cooking the tea! Where can I get one like you?

One of a kind, Heather, one of a kind. I opened the fridge door, grinning. Well, to be honest I'm heating their tea up just. I held aloft the casserole. Yankee doodle pie. Ta-ra!

She laughed. Still, you're alright, you are, loon.

I laid the dish on the table, lifted my leather jacket from the back of the chair, and got it on. Nah, I said, It's just a big act: really I'm a total bastard underneath.

But nuh. Cause if you were a bastard you wouldn't admit it, would you?

I paused in front of her, looked her in the eye. Depends how devious I was being, I suppose. She narrowed her eyes, didn't break the gaze. I screwed round my face, ending in a grin. I'm away to clean my black rotten teeth, I said, and headed for the bog.

When I got back a couple minutes later she was standing by the table, the casserole cradled in her arms. She looked down at it, made a cooing noise, and held it up at an angle towards me.

Does he not look just like his daddy?

Only if his daddy was a roll of aluminium foil.

Psh. His daddy wasn't half so useful round the house as a roll of foil.

Ah-ha, but was he as bright, that's the question.

Ha! It's a good one, Paddy. And the answer's no.

I shook my head. Well rid of him, eh Heather?

Good riddance to bad Roberts. She shrugged. Absolutely.

God, but you Torrance lassies aren't very good at keeping hold of your men. Your sister lets hers die of cancer, and yours runs away with another woman!

She looked up sharply. You are pissed off with what I said earlier. I said I was sorry.

I shrugged.

And, she went on, I've told you afore: that bastard didn't run away, I chucked him out the house!

And the band played Believe It If You Like. . .

She sighed, as if in anger, and looked at me as I zipped up my jacket. Well, I suppose this means I'm not getting a cup of coffee?

Oh! Sorry! I just forgot. I mean I am keen to get down to the old folks. But we could have one. In exchange for a lift to the village, maybe.

Nah nah, Paddy, I wasn't here to stay. I mean aye I'll give you a lift, sure, but all I was wanting was Angus's new address in Saudi off Moira. I'll get it later. It's months since I wrote to him anyway, a few more days'll make no odds.

I nodded, looked around the room. Ma got a letter from him the other day. He says it's just as bad as being stuck on a platform in the middle of the North Sea. Still no booze allowed.

Heather opened the back door and stepped out. Warmer though, she said, and shivered.

I followed, switching the kitchen light off as we went out. I closed the door, locked it, and slipped the key back under its slate on the window ledge.

See the first place any thief would look for the key? said Heather. Under that slate.

Never. The first place would be under the mat. Under the slate would be the second place, by which time the killer guard-squirrels would've ripped his throat out.

Or her throat. . .

Exactly. So watch it.

She laughed. The Beetle's down on the road, she said. I didn't want to risk it up this muddy slope here.

A few mudsplashes would do the paintjob good from what I remember.

Cheek! Are you wanting a lift or not?

Aye, aye. Great, Heather, thanks. . .

No bother, Paddy. You're alright.

Ta.

No but, *you*'re alright.

Nah!

We walked away from the house.

Doing anything exciting thenight, Heather?

Video. Just went down to the chipper in Kinker to get one: *Jacob's Ladder*, have you seen it?

Aye, it's about this window cleaner in New York, and he's got this magic A-frame that flies about to get him up to the skyscraper windows.

She laughed. Yourself, Paddy?

No, I don't have a magic ladder.

Going out on the randan are you? There's the Young Farmers' hoolie, of course.

I'll maybe put in an appearance there, right enough.

I'm sure the young ladies of the parish would be most disappointed if you didn't, Paddy.

Hih. I reckon the young ladies of the parish wouldn't notice if I turned up with a sheep under my arm and a sign on my back saying JUST MARRIED.

Patrick! You're terrible!

Life's terrible, and I'm alive, so what do you expect?

No, you're terrible as in funny, she said, after a moment.

We were passing the house's nameboard on top of its post. I waved an arm at it as we went by, before Heather had the chance to say anything more.

I'll tell you what's funny, I said. See that sign? The name of this place? The Strath. I ask you! The Strath? Daft, eh? Do you not think? Heather?

It's always been called The Strath.

I jumped ahead and turned to face her, arms spread. Aye, exactly, and what does that mean?

She paused, then sidestepped me and walked on. What do you mean what does it mean?

Strathdon, Strathtay, Strathbogie... Strath means valley! Think about it: who'd call a house on top of a hill The Valley? Mental!

We were at the car. She looked at me over the curve of the roof as we went to open our doors. Maybe it's called The Strath cause you get a good view of the whole of the den from up here.

I opened my mouth, then shut it again. Oh aye, I said. I never thought of that.

We got into the car. The seats were cold. She passed me the old folks' grub and I put it down on the rubber mat between my feet, then looked out the windscreen at the scatter of stars in the clear sky and the scatter of house lights the length of the howe. Right in the middle was the yellow glare of the Blackden streetlamps; the cluster of lights made the village look bigger than it ever did in daytime.

Heather stuck the key in the ignition, the headlights blasted out against the trees on her side of the road, and we drove off. After a second she reached for the shiftstick between us and moved it backwards to change gear. Her knuckles pressed into the side of my thigh. I remembered her catching me at the sink with my cock out, and felt my face heating up in the dark. Was the kitchen window really too dirty to see through? I couldn't be sure. Heather wrenched the stick away from me and up into third.

She glanced at me. What are you thinking about, thinker?

Eh. . . I snapped my head away from her, as if seized by a sudden need to look out the side window. I was thinking what crap names Scottish rivers have, I said.

What?

Dee? Don? The Black Burn down there? And the Spey? Spaying's something nasty you do to a cat!

Heather laughed.

My sister's got a friend in America, I went on. Ken what the river she bides by is called? The Cranberry River. You can just picture it, eh? Brilliant! You could just dive in and drink the whole thing with that name on it. What've we got here? At the back of Bennachie there's the Gadie – gads! And the Bogie. Christ, Scotland, you have to be joking: the Bogie!

She nodded, grinning. You're not a nationalist then, Patrick?

No, Aquarius.

But seriously. There's a lot of folk your age in the Party, you ken. I mean, our branch, up at Mortlich: you'd probably mind half them there from school. It's good. You should come.

23

I shrugged in the darkness. The shoulders of my leather jacket squeaked above the gurgling of the Beetle's motor.

Seriously though, Patrick. I mean, it was your birthday just before the election – eighteen years old – so who did you vote for?

Ach. . . I gazed straight ahead, didn't answer.

No, come on, she said after a few seconds. Who?

Nobody, I said. I didn't vote.

She stamped on the brakes. What! she cried, as we hurtled forward against our seatbelts.

Jesus, I'm sorry, Heather. I reached for the door-handle. Do you want me to get out and walk?

She looked at me for a second, frowning, then blinked and uncreased her forehead and said, Don't be daft. No. She let the car roll down the hill a bit, then put it into gear, and we drove on.

Not voting! she said after a while. Dear oh dear. And you know who got in, don't you? Terrible. Do you never look around you, Patrick, and think? Do you never think, God, this place is in a hell of a mess?

Aye, it could do with a bit of a redd-up, I dare say.

Look at your pals that don't have jobs. Look at the folk in the village that can't get a home: Richard and Isobel Marshall, two years married and still biding with her folks, cause they can't afford a house, cause they're all bought at great high prices by incomers to the village – incomers to the country!

You're starting to sound like a speech from parliament, Heather, if you'll excuse me being so rude. Gazing out the bottom corner of the windscreen, between the tax disc and the dashboard, I saw two dots of light flash in the undergrowth: the eyes of some beast reflecting the carlights. What was that? I turned to try and look back, but Heather drove on, still talking.

The National Party stands up for the people of Scotland, she was saying.

Aye, and for the queen, I muttered.

And on a local level it stands up for the folk of Blackden. Have you no patriotism in your body, Patrick? Don't you like this part of the world you're living in?

I turned in my seat to face front, and after a second's silence realised she really wanted an answer. Aye I like it, I said. This part of the world? I love it! I'd like to marry it! This part of the world with the Braes of Corse on one side and Ben MacDeamhain and the Aberdeen road on the other. . .aye. But once you start putting a name till it – Blackden – no! Cause that means we have to like this lump of land better than the next lump of land, cause that's called something else. Kincardine O' Corse? A townful of tinks! Kemnay? They beat us at football! Let's all go over in a couple cars and duff them up: Blackden Boot Boys versus Kemnay Casuals! Death to Kemnay!

I was talking loudly, almost shouting, and I didn't ken why. I shut up. There was silence in the car. The lights of the village were approaching. After we passed the first one I said, Well, that's what I think anyway: it's probably rubbish, as per usual.

No no, it's fine, said Heather. I mean it's a principle you've got there, and you're sticking to it. That's okay.

I sighed. Ach, it's not a principle, it's just. . .I don't know what it is. It's a feeling.

The problem with principles is, while you're so busy holding on to them, you haven't a free hand to help anyone else. And people need help, Patrick. Think about it.

We had crossed the Shakkin Briggie and were driving slowly towards the square. I'd be getting out soon.

I'd like the Scottish Nationalists more if they didn't have the word Nationalist in their title, I said. Or Scottish. That's only there to give them an excuse to slag off the English. I thought for a second. I reckon they should call it the Land and Water and Trees and Rain and Buildings Party. That way nobody gets left out.

Heather half-laughed, half-sighed, glanced in her mirror, and slowed down. Talking of getting left out, Patrick, I suppose I better put you off here.

We were coming up to my grandparents' street. Oh, great, thanks. She pulled over, and I undid my safety belt and opened the door, still sitting there. Look, I said, I feel bad about ranting away just now. In your own car as well! I'm just havering, anyway: I'm well known for it.

Political debate, Patrick, that's what it's all about. She punched me gently on the side of my leg. You should definitely come along to our next branch meeting.

Maybe I will. Aye, I will, I probably will. I got out of the car, then, I'm free! I cried, and jumped for joy. She tried to chain me to the gearstick and drag me along to vote, but I escaped!

Bye, Patrick, she said, smiling.

Bye, Auntie Heather, I said, and shut the door. See you. . .

She drove off fast, brake-lights just flickering as she approached the square, then disappearing from view.

I turned towards Albert Street, stuck my hands in my pockets, then remembered: the casserole was still on the floor of Heather's car.

For about thirty seconds I just stood there, half thinking what to do next, half hoping that Heather would maybe realise I'd forgotten the yankee doodle pie and come back with it. But it was obvious that she wouldn't, really: the casserole was hidden in the darkness of the footwell, and she'd have no reason to look there even when she got home. Probably the food would lie for weeks, till it stank so bad she'd go looking, thinking a mouse had crept in and died or something.

I had to get some grub from somewhere else, the old folks would be depending on it. I was already late, and I couldn't be bothered walking all the way back up the hill to the house. But the shops in the village had been shut for hours, and the nearest chipper was three miles away. The pub did food, bar suppers and stuff, and they'd got quite good since the place was taken over during the summer. But I could hardly go in and order and walk out with a plate in each hand, piled high.

I wouldn't need to go in the bar at all though! Ha! I headed off in the direction of the square and the Auld Mill.

There were a few cars parked outside, and the lighted signs above the Bar and Lounge entrances were shining out, but I ignored those and went down the side of the building, past the concrete cell with the gas canisters in it, till I came to the window of the hotel kitchen. I looked in. The glass was steamed up, but over at the far side of the room, whomping some kind of mallet down onto a tabletop, was Shona Findlay. She'd been a friend of my sister's all through the school years, and till Helen had buggered off south. At about that time Shona had started training with an oil company caterers, but a couple months back she'd come home to be the new chef at the Mill. I was going to knock on the window and wave, but I had visions of me doing it just as the mallet descended, and Shona getting distracted and whacking her fingers into splinters. Instead I went to the door a few paces away, pushed it open, and stepped inside.

Immediately in front of me a narrow stone staircase led steeply upwards. To my right was the kitchen door, and down the end of the corridor I could see an enormous chest freezer stuffed into a tiny dark room. The floor of the corridor was half-covered with boxes of fruit, open bags of tatties, crates of beer bottles and soft drinks. A white cat looked up from lapping in a big metal butcher's tray, empty except for puddles of bright red blood lying in the dents in its bottom. The cat stared at me. It had one green and one blue eye. I stared back. The cat blinked, then returned to licking up the blood, its tongue making quiet rasping sounds on the metal.

I took a step towards the kitchen door. The thumping from inside stopped, there was a clang, then it started again. I pushed open the door and walked in. A wave of steam, laden with smells of chip-fat, chicken juice and roasting beef, roiled over me. Opposite the door was a long gas cooker with various pots hottering away on it, lids askew. Under the window on the right was a double sink, both halves piled high with dirty dishes, trays and pans. Against the left-hand wall was a big old table, scattered with knives, rolling-pins and whisks, old margarine tubs full of chopped onions, tomatoes, lettuce, various bottles of ketchup, oil, wine, and a plastic bucket of raw chips floating in murky water. Shona was standing there, a plate of steaks on one side, the mallet in her hand. She pulled a steak off the plate onto the board in front of her, brought the mallet whamming down onto it, then gave the steak a quarter turn and hammered it again, then turned and hammered, turned and hammered. She flipped the battered steak over and did the same on the other side.

When she'd finished, she picked up the big red rag of meat, tossed it to the other end of the table onto a tray of flour and flattened steaks. She paused, wiped her nose on the sleeve of her white jacket, then pulled another of the small thick bits of meat in front of her. She raised the mallet, but waited long enough to shout, Well don't just fucking stand there! before bringing it down. Whump! What're the bastards wanting now?

Hoi, Shona, hello!

Whump! What do they want?

No, nothing. Whump! Shona, it's me, Paddy.

Whump! She let the mallet rest on the meat, and looked up towards me. Christ, Paddy! Patrick Hunter! It's been a year or two! She wiped her sleeve across her forehead, which was shiny with sweat and settled steam.

Looks like hot work, I said, stepping closer and leaning on the end of the cluttered table.

Fucking hot! But if I stripped any more I'd be fucking indecent!

Ach, you look decent enough to me. . . Eh, I mean you're looking well. I've seen you passing a couple times like, but I've never actually got the chance to say. . .anything. Till now.

I'm stuck in this fucking hole, that's why. She leant over and moved the flattened steaks around in their tray of flour. Fucking non-stop thenight too! She turned a couple of them over, patted them with floury fingertips, then picked up her mallet again. Fucking wee Drew the dishwasher, he's off fucking sick, so here's me up to my fucking eyeballs, got to do the fucking desserts and everything, and no doubt I'll have to do the fucking bastarding dishes as well afore long.

Eh, I'd offer to help, but. . .

Whump! She started hammering again. Keep well clear, Paddy, that's my advice. You're too young to die. Whump!

She was really throwing herself into it, her whole body swaying each time she brought the mallet thumping down, the tightly braided tail of black hair swinging left and right across her back.

Christ, I'm older than I used to be, I said. I mean I was just a loon last time you saw me, but that was. . . Whump!

29

And to top it all, fucking Mr John fucking Wilson said he'd do the stovies for the fucking dance in the hall. Stovies for a hundred and twenty fucking folk! Aye, he said *he*'d do them, but what he really meant was, I'll tell that dumb skivvy Shona Findlay to do them as well as every fucking other job in his minuscule antiques roadshow cunt of a kitchen!

You'd think with all the siller he spent upstairs he could've fitted this place out a bit as well.

He's all fucking show that bastard. Behind the fancy decor it's the same old shite: fucking non-stop slaving for the likes of me.

I shrugged, nodded at the steak and mallet in front of her. Don't let me keep you from your work, by the way.

She lifted the mallet and whacked it down on the lump of meat, and again, and again. I could see her grinning through the stribbles of hair falling down across her face as she bent over the table. Whump! That one was John Wilson, she said, taking the last steak off the plate at her side and getting stuck into it. Whump!

Who's this one?

Well. Whump! Who would you like it to be?

Ha! Now you're asking. Eh. . .

Whump! I was forgetting, Paddy, you've always been a peaceable kind of chiel. There's maybe nobody you'd like to see tenderized.

Tenderized? Is that what you call it? Christ, so the next time Collie and Lorna stroll in upstairs, her with a new black eye and a split lip, we've just to think, Ah, Collie's been tenderizing again. . .

Fucking dirty bastard, that man. She paused with the mallet held at shoulder height. So does Jimmy Collie get your vote then?

I nodded. Whump!

Shona grinned at me. I kent you had it in you, Paddy. Helen always said you had a vicious streak. Whump!

What? Whump!

Ha! Whump! Only joking, Paddy: she never said a bad word about you.

Aye, cause she never said any words about me. Whump!

You'd be surprised, Paddy, you'd be surprised. Whump!

There was a rushing of footsteps down the stairs and along the corridor, then the door banged open and John Wilson came running in, strode right across in front of me, and slapped several wee bits of paper on the table in front of Shona. He took a step back, smoothing down his brylcreemed hair with one hand and his tie with the other.

Fucking arse! cried Shona. You leave me twiddling my thumbs for twenty minutes then bring me three chitties in a oner! You're fucking out of order, boss!

Wilson pulled out a white cloth that was hanging from a belt-loop on his trousers, and wafted it in Shona's direction. Cool down, girl, keep cool!

She turned away from him, and lifted the tray of flattened steaks over and into the big fridge in the corner. I wish I fucking could, boss. About the only way would be to sit in this thing all night. She swung the fridge door shut with a thud. Fuck all chance of that, the way you keep me running afuckingbout.

Christ, listen, I've told you a thousand times, would you cut out language on the premises!

Who's going to fucking hear me down in the bowels?

That's not the point. I told you, we're trying to raise the tone of this place, give it a bit of style. What's the use if the staff're going around f-ing and b-ing like a bunch of schemies?

Shona glowered down at the bits of paper on the table. Anyway, you bastard, don't change the fucking subject.

Wilson sighed. I can't tell the punters when to come in the place, can I? They come in, they order, you make it. Then I. . . Christ, I can't believe this! I don't have the time to stand around talking to you! If you've a problem with the pace here tell me, and I'll find somebody who doesn't.

No problem at all, boss, no fucking problem at all. She snatched up the chitties and glanced at them in turn, then darted away across to the fridge again.

Wilson straightened himself up, tucked the cloth back into its loop, then went to walk past me. He jerked to a stop, seeming to register me for the first time. He narrowed his eyes and looked at me. Aren't you barred? he said.

What? Me?

Aye, were you not the wee toerag that pished against the public bar last month? Did I not ban you for life?

Pish against the bar? Nah! That was Stevie Begbie, he's away to the army now.

Hmm, well, alright then. He turned to walk away.

It *was* me that puked down the back of the jukebox, I said.

He spun round, a furious look all over his face.

Joke! I said, and laughed a bit.

Not funny, he said, though I could hear Shona laughing too as she worked. Wilson strode towards the door once again, stopping just as he reached it and turning to jerk his thumb at me. I want you out of here, he said. Upstairs spending, okay, but this isn't a talking-shop down here. Fuck off. He pushed out the door and was gone.

Nice guy, eh? said Shona.

Typical fucking Glaswegian bastard. . .

He's from Edinburgh.

Ah well, same difference.

Shona pushed past me with a frying pan in her hand, and started dropping handfuls of stuff into it from the spread of tubs on the tabletop. Eh, listen, Paddy, it's grand to talk to you and that, but I really am having to hash on here, so. . .

Aye, I'll just go, I've got to. . .fuck, I forgot why I came in in the first place! It's an emergency, I need a favour, Shona.

As long as it's a quick one, Paddy, she said from over at the cooker. She turned a knob, and a bulb of blue flame appeared under the pan.

Aye, it's just, I need some grub for my poor starving gran and granda, just a couple mince pies or something. I'm supposed to be taking their tea round thenight, but I don't have anything to give them.

Mince pies? she said, shaking the contents of the frying pan over the heat. You don't get stuff like that at the Auld Mill Inn these days! Cordon bleu, you cunt, take it or leave it!

Well, anything, anything at all. It's an emergency.

Let's see. . . Go into that fridge there, and you'll see some pies on the middle shelf, polystyrene cases: flaky pastry on top, prawns and fish and a pink sauce inside. Take a couple of those and disappear afore anyone sees you.

I did as she said, the first part. Eh, can I heat them up?

Fuck's sake! She came running over, took the pies out of my hands, stepped over to the other side of the room, and stuck them inside one of the microwave ovens there. She pressed something, the microwave beeped, and she hurried back to the stove. Two minutes, she said, Then bugger off out of here!

Thanks, Shona. You're a lifesaver, really.

Just for fuck's sake don't let Wilson see the pies, please.

There's some carrier-bags in the drawer by the door, stick them in there.

I went over and got a bag. The microwave beeped again, and its light went out. I opened the door and slid the pies into the bag, hot cod's breath puffing up into my face as the pastry lid on one of the pies shifted slightly. That's me off then, I said, heading for the door. Thanks again.

Cheerio, Paddy, she said, amongst a rattle of pots. Maybe see you at the dance later, eh? I'll be over with the fucking stovies, anyway.

Definitely, I said, Definitely see you there. It's great to talk to you again, Shona, very good indeed. I was all ready to give her a big grin and a wink as I backed out the door, maybe fix a time to see her later, buy her a drink in return for the pies. . .but she was totally caught up in the cooking and didn't look round.

Across the square from the pub there were lights on in Wolfe the butcher's. This wasn't unusual: after thirty years he's still working late trying to become the world's first mealie-pudding millionaire. As I watched, the man himself appeared in the window, unhooked a line of chops and a leg of lamb from the bar there, and disappeared again. I lifted the pies so I was holding one case in each hand, and set off. The heat worked its way through the polystyrene cases and the plasic bag and burnt into my skin; within ten seconds it was unbearable. I set the bag down on the steps of the Queen Victoria fountain in the middle of the square and waved my hands around in the cool air above my head, jigging from foot to foot with the pain.

The butcher reappeared and started wiping the inside of his

window with a cloth. After a couple dichts he stopped, cupped his hand around his eyes, and peered out into the square, face squashed against the glass so his nose was turned up at the end. It made him look more like a pig than a wolf. Sometimes he looked awfully like a sheep – with his tight-curled white hair and his bushy white sideburns – but tonight he definitely looked like a pig. After watching me for a few seconds, he raised his free hand, tapped the side of his forehead, and pointed at me.

I stopped dancing around and blew on my palms instead.

Wolfe went back to work; producing a scroll of orange paper from somewhere, he flattened it out against the glass and started securing the corners with sellotape. I picked up the bag of pies by the handles and went a few steps closer. The notice had a glaikit looking turkey printed on it, and lettering saying: ORDER EARLY THIS XMAS! A BIRD IN THE "BOOK" IS WORTH TWO IN THE "BUSH"! I walked on past the window and up the road towards my grandparents' street.

I kent Wolfe wouldn't be getting my family's business this christmas. Last year there'd been a bit of a mix up that had ended in what my ma reckoned was the biggest disaster ever. What happened was, she thought she'd ordered a stuffed turkey, so when we sat down – her, my sister, me, my gran and granda – with plates of sprouts, tatties, chippolatas and gravy, and my ma sliced open the bird, we were all expecting oatmeal and onion to come gushing out the arse of the thing. Instead all that appeared was a half-melted plastic bag of neck, queern, heart and liver. Ma was completely dumbfounded – she just stood there, her mouth open, looking madder and madder. My sister swore; my granda laughed; my gran asked if this was boil-in-the-bag. I said nothing. I couldn't get too worked up about it somehow, this blood and guts spilling out amongst the tinsel and crackers. I quite liked it, it seemed more honest: a heart and a liver are the kind of things that are supposed to be inside a turkey, and it was good to be reminded of real life in the middle of christmas day. But my ma didn't take that view of it. She'd had to go back to Wolfe's since, cause there wasn't another butcher for ten miles. But she'd already placed an order with a place in Aberdeen for this year's turkey.

I walked on, back the way I'd come only twenty minutes before. There was hardly anybody about, except for a few folk moving around inside their houses. It was hard not to look at them as I passed, what with them all brightly lit through open curtains, and me davering along in the dark.

A car was approaching from out of town at high speed, its headlight-beams bouncing in the branches of the roadside trees as it came in over the head of the north-end hill, then bearing in on me as it accelerated down the long straight towards the square. It flashed past. I blinked its lights out of my eyes, walking blind for a second. Behind me the car's brakes were screeching, and almost immediately the gears crunched and the engine whined into a high-speed reverse. It shot past me backwards and stopped: a patched-up white Capri, Brian Milne's. I walked up to it and crouched to look in the open passenger's window.

I hope you realise you were speeding there, I said.

Aye aye, man, said Bri from the driver's seat.

Speeding? said Jock the Cock beside him. We never touched any drugs. . .

What! I rolled my eyes. You're letting Brian fucking mentaller Milne drive you about without the aid of anaesthetics? Brave man!

Jock the Cock laughed. Or stupid.

Who're you calling stupid? said Bri. And what's all this about drugs?

36

He's calling himself stupid, I said.

First sensible thing he's said all day then.

But he's calling you mental, said Jock.

I give up, said Bri. It's you that's mental, Cock-o. Or else maybe that's where the drugs come in, I don't know. . .

Everybody laughed.

What's going on, anyway? I said.

Well, I was meant to be getting a lift home from young Brian here, said Jock the Cock. But as you can see we seem to have come to an unscheduled stop several hundred metres short of the target. And the question is, why? Has the Casanova of Nether Craigton spotted – sniffed out, even – some fresh new talent in the vicinity, and is even now preparing to boot me out, drag her in, and set the seats for maximum recline?

Or has he just got scunnered of your yapping, you cunt, said Bri, And he's about to boot you out just for the hell of it?

Let's hope it's the latter, went on Jock, twisting his London accent into something only half a million miles away from a BBCer. Cause any female catching sight of the amount of cataloid on the old Ford phallic symbol here is likely to conclude that young Craigton's supply of condoms has been repeatedly patched with his bicycle repair kit!

I don't ken what the fuck you're talking about, said Bri as I laughed, But you're right about one thing: I am booting you out just for the hell of it!

Jock gaped at him, then turned to me in appeal, his eyes bigger than a kicked dog's. Listen to that, he said. Your friend's about to throw his poor crippled workmate out into the gutter! Me with my knees burned off and everything.

Get to fuck you glumshie bastard, said Bri. That wasn't what we were hearing when you started in on those massive fucking wages!

If that's the way you feel, I'll get out and crawl my painful way home alone, said Jock, and opened the car door. He paused, one leg out. Well, what do you say?

Bri grinned. I never said nothing, Jock. I definitely never said bide in the car.

I grabbed the top of Jock's arm and hauled him up out of the carseat. He hobbled around on the pavement for a second, putting on the big limps.

Fuck off! shouted Bri from inside the car.

Jock started off down the street, still crippling away, though not so over the top now.

Here, Cock-o, I cried. Some day your legs are going to get ripped off by wild dogs or your kids or something, and none of us'll fucking believe it, cause you've tried it on so many times!

He raised a hand over his shoulder: the prongs. Then he turned and walked backwards, grinning. Thanks for the lift, Bri, he said, and turned the prongs into thumbs-up. See yous later. He jumped in the air, knocked his heels together, then ran off across the square towards his house along the Kinker road.

I crouched down on the pavement again to talk to Bri through the open car door. Man's a chancer, I said.

Man's a pain in the fucking neck, said Bri, shaking his head. Christ, he was bad enough before the Piper Alpha thing, but ever since he's been ten times worse!

It can't've been fun.

No, but I reckon it was the best thing that ever happened to Jock the Cock: gave him something to fucking moan about for the rest of his life.

Been up at your place all day has he? I can see the signs of overexposure to the cockney wit and wisdom.

Bri nodded. I don't ken why my dad keeps taking him on

every time he needs extra help; he's useless, he's. . .

Here, hold on a minute Bri, I broke in. I've just remembered: I've got this grub here, I've got to take it round to my gran and granda for their tea. While it's still hot, like. So. . .

Aye, fair enough, said Bri, looking a bit disgruntled at me shutting him up all the same. Are you wanting a. . .no, fuck that: I've given enough lifts theday, I'm needing a pint!

I'm only going round the corner, I said. I'll not be long. Tell you what, get me a pint and I'll be back for it in ten minutes. I said to Dek I'd probably see him afore the Young Farmers' do. . .

Bri reached over and pulled the car door shut in front of my face. Dekkie's in there already, he said. We just about run him over in the square thenow. Ha! The bastard was scampering about like a fucking rattan, and here's me trying to get from sixty to zero without skidding into the fucking fountain!

Bri wound the passenger window closed to all but a couple of cm. I put my mouth to the gap and said, You never know your luck: you might just catch Jock instead if you put your foot down!

Ten minutes then, said Bri, and pulled away, tyres squeaking. I turned and walked in the opposite direction. Fast, but not fast enough for my Docs to screel on the pavement.

I headed up to the old folks' house. From the outside it looks more like a shed than a house. It's set right up against the back wall in the garden of one of the big Victorian places along Albert Street. The way it's hidden from the big house's windows by a row of bushes makes it seem like a place you'd stash your barrows and rakes in, rather than a couple of eighty-year-olds. Only the chimneys are made of stone; the walls are green-painted wood, the roof red corrugated-iron. If you're sitting inside and the rain comes on, it sounds like the whole drum section of the Gordon Highlanders Regimental Pipe Band is rattling over your head. But it faces south and the fires heat the wee rooms fine and warm in no time at all. It's called the Summer House.

I went along the narrow path down the side of the big garden, paused for a second to transfer the bag of pies to my left hand, then thumped on the door and walked straight in, calling out, Aye aye! It's Paddy! as I closed the door behind me.

Come away in, called my granda's voice from the living-room. I crossed the scullery and stuck my arm with the bag of pies dangling from the end of it through the doorway curtain.

Fresh fish pies! I cried. Hot from the hotel ovens: stappit full of goodness and grease and goodness knows what!

My granda chuckled. Show your face, pieman. Show your pies as well.

I drew back my arm and pushed my head through the curtains, grinning. Aye aye, granda, I said.

Aye, loon, what like? He leant back in his chair by the fire and looked up at me.

I'm fine, fine. But listen, I've got your tea here. You better eat it afore it's cold.

He lifted a hand from the arm of his chair and waved it towards the scullery. There's plates set out, he said.

I ducked back through the curtain, found the two plates lying there, and shuffled a pie out of the bag onto each. There were knives and forks lying on the worktop too, and cups and saucers. I flipped the pies out of their polystyrene cases, put them back the right way up, and swept away a few stray flakes of pastry. Then I took the plates through to the room and gave one to my granda.

Thankyou, sir, he said, and plunged his fork through the lid of the pie.

I was still standing. What'll I do with Gran's?

He lifted a forkful of fish and pastry to his mouth, holding the plate close under his chin with the other hand. By heaven, this hasn't come too soon, he said, chewing away.

Aye, I'm sorry I'm a bittie late with it, Granda. You must be starving.

Och, I've no hunger at all these days, he said, stoking in another big forkload. I've been peching for a smoke since the back of one, that's all.

For what? I don't ken if it's smoked fish or. . .

Ho! No loon, for a rick on my pipe. My last one was after my dinner at half-twelve, and once I've finished this I'll have another. That's all I'm allowed these days. He dug his fork about in the depths of the pie, speared something, and pulled it out, wagging it at me as he carried it to his mouth. Ken this, Paddy, I don't believe I'd bother eating at all these days if I wasn't looking forward to my pipe at the end of it.

I shook my head. Dearie dear, Granda: unhealthy stuff that, you ken. You'll be cut down in your prime if you carry on with that habit.

He laughed through a mouthful of pie, swallowed, and said, Havers, loon! I've smoked an ounce of the Bogie Roll every week since I was fourteen, and it's never become a habit yet.

I was still standing there with a pie on a plate, while my gran was probably dying of hunger ben the house. Listen, I said, What'll I do with this? Will I take it through? It's getting cold.

Set it down by the fire then. He pointed with the toe of his baffie to the far side of the grate where there was a pile of logs. I balanced the plate on top of the pile and sat down in the seat

41

opposite him, my gran's seat. Lying on the arm of it were a couple knitting needles stuck into a ball of wool, with a fragment of jersey or scarf underneath, loose ends hanging down.

It's like the Marie Celeste, this chair, I said.

What?

Och. . .nothing. Somebody I kent at school. I watched him finish chewing, wipe some sauce from around his mouth. How long is it since she's been through now?

Hmm. He looked into the fire; it was burning low.

A month or so, is it? He said nothing. Five weeks?

He cleared his throat. Hoy on another log, will you, loon?

I lifted the plate with my gran's pie on it and took up the top log, a wedge of yellow pine with a crust of girsley bark down one side. The top of the logpile was uneven now, and I couldn't set the plate back down, so I kept a hold of it while I lodged the wood on top of the half-burnt and burning stuff in the grate. Yellow flames began to leaf up around its edges; there was a faint sizzling; the smell of resin reached my nose.

That's a fine sweet reek, I said.

It's a rare perfume, pine sap in the fire, he said. But I still get the shivers down my back any time I smell it. He gazed into the fire, then looked up at me, his eyes glinting.

I pushed back my sleeve and looked at my watch. I should really be getting on, Granda, I said. I'm meant to be meeting a couple folk.

The shivers! he cried again, and set his hands trembling so that the fork went skittling across his empty plate.

I laughed.

He looked at me from under lowered brows.

How's that, Granda? I said.

He smiled, set his plate down on the floor, and leant back in his chair. I put Gran's plate down too, on the tiled area right in front of the fire, and sat back in her chair, the wings of it coming out on each side of my head, directing my gaze across to my granda.

It was in the war, Paddy, the last war, and I was exempt and working in the timber up at the Forest of Birse. And me and your mother, your granny I mean, we bade in a cottage in the grounds of Ballogie House. One black night, a spail of a moon in the sky just, a Gerry bomber overshot Aberdeen completely, missed the docks or whatever he'd been after, and ended way away up Deeside. And there were hills he'd never reckoned on meeting! But meet them he did, head on too, at a fair old rate of knots. He went right into the side of a thing we called the Bogieshiel Brae, right into the trees there at top speed and scythed a great swathe of them down with his wings. We could hear the thundering of the crash from inside the house, and by the time we got to the door, what did we see but the whole side of the brae lit up by the explosion, the sight of it first and then the sound of it, the force of the sound pressing us back against the doorpost. By heaven, we thought the whole hill was tumbling down on top of us!

He slapped a hand against the side of his chair, laughed.

You must've thought it was a volcano bursting out the top of Bogieshiel, eh?

Well, we kent fine it had been a plane going over, a big one maybe by the drone of it, but we didn't find out till later it was a Gerry one, and we never were told for sure it was carrying incendiary bombs, though it must've been: we could see the fires it started with our own een! There was thirty seconds of silence after the first explosion, then more bangs and booms, and these great spouts of fire went shooting up, way over the tops of the trees on each side. A big red hand of fire reaching up into the darkness, that's what it looked like. And then it came down. The hand came reaching down towards us, the fingers of the fire stretching out over the woods in all directions towards Ballogie, and setting the timber ablaze wherever it touched. And the noise it made was like a hundred steam-engines roaring and crackling down the brae straight for our cottage in its wee clearing in the trees. And nearer it came, nearer, the hand was closing in about us, your granny and me, it was closing its fingers, tighter, tighter. And there was a different sound now underneath the roaring, it was a hissing and a spitting, the sap of the pines bursting out of the boughs and trunks as it boiled. It sent cones fizzing into the air like rockets, whole branches flying off in flames. . .

He was gripping the arms of his chair, broad fingers pressing deep into the cushioning, eyes wide and flickering in the flamelight from the fireplace.

Scary, I said. He showed no signs of hearing.

And that was when the smell of it came too. I mind turning to Mary – the two of us still standing there in the doorway, it had happened so fast – I turned to her, opened my mouth to say something, goodbye maybe, and the blaze was that close that the air felt burning in my throat. And thick too – hot air, thick and sweet and choking with the reek of the roasting pinesap. I mind thinking to myself, This'll be us away to die then, what a rare smell that resin has! But then, just as I thought that, just as the last thing I was ever going to think went through my head, something happened. The fingers of the fire seemed to loosen their grip a bit, they seemed to move back and sideways away from our clearing. . . Inside a minute we could see it plain. The wind had swung round from the west to the south, and the smoke was clearing from about us. The hand of the fire was moving away northwards, slowly at first, then speeding again, till it was roaring loud in the crowns of the larch plantation, off up the hill and over the other side in the direction of Balfour. And then I kent that we were safe, and the thing would surely burn itself out by dawn, for I'd been over above Balfour with the squad only the week afore cutting a system of fine wide breaks on the slope there. But for a minutie. . .

He paused, and for a while neither of us spoke, we both just sat there watching the logs in the grate. They were burning away as quiet and even as a cat purring.

It took weeks for the reek of the burnt resin to go from the house and our clothes, my granda said at last. And ken this, I don't think it's ever gone from my mind.

God aye, I said. I'm surprised you haven't switched to smokeless fuel long syne!

He chuckled to himself, looked into the fire, then reached into the middle of it with the toe of his baffie to shift the topmost chunk of pine further back into the blaze. But there's nothing like it for a heat on a cold night, he said. Even if it does give me the shivers from time to time!

Ach aye. I sat up in the chair. Talking of cold nights, Granda, I better get out into this one, or my pals'll think I've gone home to my bed.

Aye aye, loon. Very good. But listen. . . He looked away from the fire and nodded in the direction of the bedroom. Would you put your head round the door and say hello to your granny afore you go? She hasn't seen anybody all day.

Och, okay. Sure. I'd like to. I bent over to lift her plate from the fireplace; the edge nearest me was cool, but the side near the fire was burning hot. Ow! I jerked my fingers away and waved them in the air.

Ho! Watch it, loon! You have to be careful with the fire, you ken!

I sucked my burnt fingertips in my mouth for a second, then took them out to wave them about again and say, Is that the moral to your story then, Granda? Watch and not burn your fingers when you're close to the fire?

The moral? Ach no, I don't think it. I'm not much of a one for morals, I just tell the tale. Work out a moral for yourself if you want one!

We both laughed. I got to my feet. I'll go through then, say hello. Then I really should skedaddle.

I'll be right after you, said my granda, inching forwards in his chair, getting ready to stand up. I'll maybe make her a cup of tea to go with it.

I crossed the room to the door, went through into the tiny lobby with the toilet off it, then tapped on the next door and went into the bedroom.

A wall of warm, worn-out air met me as I stepped in. It was dark too, the only light coming from a small lamp with a scarf of some green material draped over its shade on a chest of drawers to one side of the bed. Towards the other side of the bed lay my gran. The covers were pulled up over her chest and arms to her shoulders, but her head was propped high on several pillows. It gave her a strange look, especially with the greenish light from the side shining on the tight skin of her cheekbone and her brow and the ridge of her nose. Her eyes were closed, her face was absolutely still; my heart suddenly clunked against my ribs.

Gran!

She opened her eyes and was looking straight at me, smiling. Patrick! Are you alright, laddie?

Aye, aye! Eh, aye. I was just, it's just. . .you're looking awfully thin, Gran.

She smiled again. I haven't got my teeth in, she said.

46

Oh, your teeth. . .

She frowned, her head shifting slightly on the pillows. Are you sure you're alright, my dear? You look a bit pale.

I nodded. I'm fine.

Her shoulder moved. Sit down here a whilie.

I sat down on the side of the bed. It's a few weeks since I saw you, Gran. Not since that time I visited you at the hospital, mind. Not long after they took you in.

Oh, did you visit me, Patrick? My memory's a bittie hazy around then to be honest. But I believe you were there, aye, you were indeed. That was good of you.

Don't be daft, Gran.

But you're back now, that's the main thing, you're back to see me again. She smiled at me; I smiled back.

I brought you your supper, Gran, your tea.

Oh, that's nice. Did you catch it yourself?

What? Catch it? Well I bought it. . .eh, I got it myself from the hotel.

That's nice of you, Patrick, very nice.

Fish pie. Granda's just taking it through to you in a minute. But I thought I'd look in first, afore I go, ken.

You're not going already are you, Patrick? You've only just got here!

Hih, Gran, I've been through there for hours, that's the thing, and I'm meant to be meeting my pals. Granda was telling me one of his stories: about you and him caught in a forest fire, up at Ballogie.

Her thin eyebrows angled into a frown. A fire? she said after a second.

Aye, during the war. A big forest fire up at Ballogie, and you thought you were going to get. . .hih. A plane started it.

Her head moved on the pillows: a shake. It's funny, Patrick, I don't mind a fire up there at all. Sometimes I think my mind's going. She paused. Mind you, sometimes I think your granda's is. Just the other day he was telling me he remembered the night the Tay Bridge blew down! I said to him, I know you're an old timer, Jamie, but you're not that old surely! He-he!

I laughed a bit too, then moved sideways till I was almost off the bed. I took a deep breath to say goodbye with.

I walked into the bar. Jock the Cock glanced round from aiming at the dartboard, turned himself to face the door and started aiming at my forehead.

Here, Paddy.

What?

Wingnut here says he seen you getting a ride off some tasty blonde bird.

What? I looked over at Jock's mate, who was leaning on the end of the bar, fiddling with his dart flights.

Well, a ride in her car, anyway.

What, theday? What shite's this, Wingy?

He didn't answer. Wingnut hardly ever spoke to anyone except Jock the Cock; instead his face just went red whenever you tried to take him on. It was doing that now, and he was staring at his darts and poking at them as they lay across the palm of his big red hand.

Sure it was today, Jock went on. Christ, Paddy, it was just an hour or two ago. Your tadge must still be steaming!

I rolled my eyes. Ach, that'll've been my auntie. She did give me a lift down here earlier on.

Your auntie? Don't give us it!

It's right enough: my auntie Heather.

Wingnut says it was some young blonde, a nice looker.

We both looked at Wingnut. His lugs stuck out from the side of his head, and they looked very red with the gantry lights behind them. He closed his lips tighter, stuck his stubbly chin out, said nothing.

Come on, Paddy, said Jock. Who's this secret bit of stuff? None of this old auntie crap!

I don't ken what age she is: thirty or something I suppose. She's my mother's wee sister, like, a good bit younger.

Eh? Come on!

Sorry to disappoint you, Cocky.

Fuck me. . .your auntie? He turned back to the board, launched a dart in its general direction.

Double three, said Wingnut, and immediately looked down at his own darts again.

That's you putting him off with your non-stop yapping, Wingy, I said.

Leave him alone, said Jock, and chucked his last two darts at the board one after the other.

Twentyseven total, said Wingnut.

Just my age, said Jock, striding up to the board and snatching his darts out of the cork. Here. . . He turned and walked right up to me, while Wingnut lined up to throw. Is this straight about your auntie?

Aye, my auntie Heather. She lives out on the Corse House estate.

I get it, your old lady's sister. He nodded. So were you giving her a sly poke, were you?

Fuck's sake, Cocky! You're sick, you cunt!

49

What? Nah: stony broke, that's what I am. And I'll tell you one good thing about incest: at least it saves on travelling expenses!

Ach, that's it, you bastard, I'm off. You're a fucking perv man!

One hundred and forty! called Wingnut.

And another thing, I said. You're married, you can't spend much travelling expenses rolling from one side of the bed to the other!

But I'm talking about sex, son, not marriage. There's a fuck of a difference.

I wouldn't know.

Say no more, son, say no more. He turned back to the board, the ends of his moustache twitching as he grinned, to continue getting slaughtered by Wingy.

I looked around the bar, meanwhile wondering to myself whether Wingnut's lugs operated as some kind of radar maybe, with his beamer face pulsing out infra-red beams to be picked up and used in direction-finding while playing darts. . .

I made my way to the far end of the bar, where Mhairi was leaning drinking a cup of coffee and reading the *Evening Express*.

Quiet thenight, Mhairi.

She looked up. It was busy earlier on, but everybody's gone along the road, I reckon. She shrugged, took a sip of coffee. Including Wilson, otherwise I wouldn't be having this outwith my official ten-minute break, would I?

When the cat's away, eh?

The barstaff return to their bad old habits. Jings, I'll be serving folk drinks on the slate next!

Christ, that is an old habit. Before my time, that one. Mind you, I've only been coming here ninetynine years.

She wrinkled her nose. It was her way of smiling. So what are you going to order to make me earn my paltry wages, then?

Poultry wages? I said, shimmying my shoulders. Does that mean you get paid chicken feed?

Right Hunter, you're barred. Her nose was wrinkling again.

That's okay, I said, Cause I wasn't actually needing a drink. She slumped back down on the bar, picked up her mug. I was just wondering if Dek and Brian were here. Seen them, have you?

Mhairi nodded, drinking coffee. But they left ages ago, quarter to nine or something. They were cursing you out actually. Dek'd bought you a pint then you never showed up.

Shit! Is it still about then?

You're joking! They split it atween them, then they went off. Along to the dance I think.

I nodded. Aye, likely. I leant off the bartop. Well thanks, Mhairi. See you later.

You could look in the lounge.

Nah, there's as much chance of finding them there as there is of Jock winning the darts tourney, I said, as I walked down the length of the bar.

What's that you're saying about me? Jock put in as I passed him.

I was saying you've the biggest pizzle this side of the mannie Milne's Charolais bull.

Hey, what's new? said Jock, spreading his hands out to Wingnut, who went red in the face and giggled.

I pushed open the door.

Here, Paddy, Jock shouted after me. Mention that fact to your auntie next time you meet up. I'm getting the hots just hearing about her!

I went on out.

*

51

The jubilee clock on the hall tower was at ten o'clock. The dance had been going on for a good two hours. I paid my one-fifty at the door, got BYF stamped on the back of my hand in purple ink, and went into the main hall. The band was playing a waltz with yodelling, and the whole place was a mess of couples stepping and shuffling about, the good dancers straight-faced, the clumsy ones tripping over each other's feet and laughing to cover it up. The laughing and the thumping of the feet was loud, and the music was louder: keyboard, accordion and guitar. The big singer let rip a yodelling solo. When he went up onto the high notes the speakers squealed and it felt like somebody was pressing the sharp end of a pencil against my eardrums.

I looked around the hall. Dek and Bri were sitting at a small table halfway along the far wall. Later on they'd probably get to dancing, but that would require a few more drinks down the throat. Skirting the edge of the dance area, I made my way across the hall towards them.

Their backs were to the wall. They spotted me and raised their half-empty glasses in salute.

Aye aye! called Bri.

It's the disappearing man, said Dek.

I stopped, standing by the table. Is this seat somebody's?

Aye, it's the council's, said Bri. The whole place is.

I sat down.

You can't sit there, said Dek. That seat's reserved for the late Mr Patrick Hunter, the very late Mr Hunter! So late in fact that his pals waiting in the fucking boozer came to the solution he'd been struck dead by a bolt of lightning and was never going to turn up ever so they keep that seat empty in eternal remembrance of the cunt!

That's alright then, I said, Cause I just seen the boy Hunter, and he said I could have his seat till he turned up.

You'll be there all night, likely, said Dek.

We all laughed, and Bri and Dek took a drink out of their beer. I felt in my jacket pocket for my wallet, thick with the week's pay.

Where've you been anyway, you bugger? asked Bri. I thought you were just coming.

Ach, it's a long story. Not to be told on a dry mouth. Are you needing a. . .

Dek was already on his feet, and edging out from behind the table. I'll get this one: it was my round, you can catch up.

I stood my hand along at the Mill, said Bri.

So I heard.

Aye, but it evaporated afore you got to it, said Dek, and zigzagged away from the table into the thick of the dancers.

I nodded at nothing for a second. Bri's gaze moved round the hall, then back to me. I got held up at the old folks', I said. Ken what it's like: my granda gets started in on one of his stories, and that's you for six hours. Bri sniffed, took a drink. Interesting though. He was telling me about this massive forest fire up at Ballogie.

Bri started. What! Ballogie? Theday? I never heard about that!

Hih. I shook my head. No, this was at the time of the war: ancient history, Bri.

Christ, just as well! I thought I didn't see that on the news.

No, you wouldn't've: no telly in those days. Anyway, that's it, sorry about not making it to the Mill and that, but blood's thicker than water, ken, all that shite.

Bri blinked, drank. Not to worry, Paddy, you don't have to tell me about fucking family ties.

I mean, I like fine seeing them. . .

No, it's okay though, Paddy: we just split your pint atween us

53

and came on down here anyway. We kent you'd find us. We couldn't exactly've gone far, eh!

I half-swivelled in my chair and looked around the dancers and the scattering of folk sitting talking and drinking and smoking at the tables ranged round the edges of the hall. Most of them were from the Young Farmers' Club here, or others nearby, but there was a fair sprinkling of older folk as well.

Good turn out, I said, but as I spoke the singer came in bawling again and drowned me out.

What? shouted Bri, leaning over the table.

Fair steer of folk! I shouted towards him, but I could see from his face that he hadn't made me out. I got up and shifted round so I was sitting on the bench next to him, looking out into the centre of the hall. Big steer! I shouted again. He nodded.

Not big enough though, he yelled into my lug.

How?

No new talent! He stuck both hands into thumbs-down, and put on a miserable expression.

I scanned the crowd. I kent almost everybody from other dances in the area, or pubs; half of them I'd been at school with.

Same old faces. . . I said at the top of my voice.

Bri picked up his glass and took a big drink. Then, grinning, he said, Well, a few more pints and even the boring old faces'll look good enough to suck my you know what.

I curled my lip. That's not luck, I said, That's a fucking miracle you're after! he laughed. What's good luck, I went on, is if one of the dames gets pished enough to think you look worth a dance – never mind anything else!

Bri patted the table beside where my hand was resting. That's where you're going astray, my loon. You'll be sitting here for years if you're waiting for some lassie to invite you into her pants. It's up to you, Paddy.

Well, I don't ken about that.

Bri finished his drink, then nodded at the empty glass. Aye, it's magic stuff right enough, and the world would just seize up without it. . .

Well, Blackden would!

. . .but in the end it's more about balls than booze.

Aye, I mean look at King Charlie, your charolais. He never touches a drop, but you could put him into a park of nice-looking young cows and he'd service fifty a day, I bet.

Bri didn't laugh. Oh, fifty easy, he said.

The band stopped. The dancers stood and clapped. Through the middle of them came Dek, a pint in his hand. I stood up to let him get to his old place. The band struck up a quieter tune, an instrumental. I sat down in the seat with my back to the hall, and Dek edged past, setting a pint of headless heavy on the table in front of me.

What's this? he said, sitting. Musical fucking chairs?

I was keeping it warm for you. Cheers!

He farts like a blowtorch, said Bri, and laughed.

Next time I need any paint stripped I'll ken where to come.

The beer tasted a bittie sour, but I swallowed my mouthful anyway and was away to speak, when something behind me caught Bri's eye, and he came in with, Hey, talking of stripping. . .who's the dame in the black dress?

Dek shifted his gaze out onto the dancefloor, and I turned to look too. Everyone was in a big circle, taking a few steps forward then another few back then one or two forward then beginning again. Actually it was two circles: a big one on the outside made up of all the men, and a slightly smaller one inside, connected by some special arrangement of arms around shoulders and waists; this circle had all the women in it.

Who're you talking about? said Dek, scanning the dancers, I can't see. . .

Ach, she's hidden now behind. . .hold on till they. . .there!

He nodded quarter of the way round the circle. Just coming into view again, after being hidden by the tall guy she was linked to, was a woman I'd never seen before. After three or four teenage years in a place the size of Blackden, you can recognise any of the female population in an instant, front on, sideways, even from behind like now.

Well well, said Dek. Promising.

Her hair was blonde and shiny in the band's lights, and cut in a straight line across her shoulders like the blade of a shovel. She'd on a short black dress with black tights and bare arms.

Bags first dance, lads, said Bri.

Fair enough, said Dek, But I bags first ride.

Who is she? I said. The circle was working its way round, and she was directly across the hall now. Inbetween the couples passing just in front of us I could see her quite clearly, make out pearl earrings and necklace. She's not from these parts, anyway.

She's a bittie older, maybe, when you see her face on.

Who cares about her face, said Bri. Are the hairs on her fud grey, that's my limit.

Christ, it's good to see romance isn't dead, I said, but the others waved their hands at me.

Wheesht! Here she comes again!

We watched as the woman stepped forwards and back, forwards, forwards and back, as she moved through the portion of the circle closest to our table. She was saying something to the tall guy in the tweed jacket she was dancing with, and he was laughing. Disconnected words in an English or southern accent floated over the accordion. She danced on by.

Thirty, maybe? said Dek.

Just at her sexual peak, said Bri. And so am I!

Fuck's sake, I said. You're made for each other.

Christ aye, that guy she's with, do you reckon he's her father? He's way too old for her! Must be forty at least!

Never seen him afore either, said Dek. You'd remember a tall cunt like that.

The accordion tune came to an end, and there was a splatter of applause, including from the woman in black and her partner. He was clapping loud enough to single out – his hands must've been like paddles – and she was taking wee leaps into the air as she clapped, smiling. Then the band announced a change of tempo and launched into a country song, and the two of them turned to leave the floor.

Immediately Bri leapt to his feet. Watch this, lads, he said, and strode off at high speed across the hall directly towards the couple, pulling his sweatshirt straight and wiping his palms on the sides of his jeans as he went.

Fucking Bri doesn't waste any time! I said.

He'd reached the couple, said something, and they'd both turned and looked at him, smiling after a second.

Here comes the redder, said Dek, shaking his head.

But she followed him out onto the middle of the floor and they started dancing a kind of jive, coming in close then separating then moving in again, closer this time.

Aye, that's what you have to do, I said, Just fucking take the plunge. Not consider the ifs and buts, just fucking go for it. I sighed. That's my problem: I think about it too much, then end up doing fuck all.

Ah well, that's Bri's advantage then: thinking doesn't exactly come naturally to him, does it.

Hih. . .

We watched them. They both moved with the music, and smoothly.

He is a good dancer though.

Plenty of practice with the sheep, said Dek, and took a drink.

I laughed into my drink. What? Dancing sheep?

Christ aye, said Dek. They're well trained, the sheep at Craigton: three hundred years of Milnes shagging away. . . dancing, foreplay, you name it. Evolution, Paddy, that's what it is, survival of the best fit. Here, word has it there's one yearling yowe even gets you a glass of water and a fag afterwards!

Nah!

Aye!

Never: Bri doesn't smoke. . .

We both laughed, then turned back to watch him dancing.

The next song was a country one too: Hey Good Looking.

Fuck, said Dek. I was planning on breaking in after the second number, But I've no chance now. This is the ideal song for ten easy chat-up lines, starting with, Hey, they're singing about you, beautiful. . . I'm fucked.

Or not.

Ekfuckingxactly.

But soon the song was ending, the woman was going towards a table on the far side of the hall near the stage, and Bri came back to us, sweating and grinning. He sat down.

Well?

You smug bastard!

He looked at both of us, reached out for my pint, downed the last quarter of it in a oner, then opened his hands on the table.

Here! I said.

Wheesht, said Dek.

She's married, said Bri. Turns out that lanky cunt's her husband. And not even a trace of a scunner with him. Not even a hint of nipping outside for a sly one in the back of the shagging-wagon.

Terrible.

Bit of a wasted effort all that dancing then, I said

Damn the bit of it! Better than watching one of Dek's horny videos any day. I just about came in my breeks during that last number.

That would've impressed her, Cassanova Pish-your-pants!

Who are they, anyroad? Not on holiday in fucking November, surely? I took my glass back from in front of Bri and peered into it. Not a drop remained.

Nah, seems they're moving here from down south; she told me the place, but I've never heard of it. Queenie-something. He wiped a shower of sweat from his forehead. Brindle her name is, or – ha! – Marjorie, as her friends call her.

Brindle? The name meant something to me. Oh aye! They're the folk who've bought Dod Goodman's place off the denside road. Christ, that's them, the Brindles.

Dek wrinkled his face up. They don't look like crofting folk to me.

Nah, they're selling the whole place off, all the goods and gear, and all the parks they're leasing out. I'm working up there themorn. The roup, ken.

I'd bid a week's wages for one night with Marj, said Dek. If I was getting a wage, like.

Fuck's sake, I said. Desperate or what?

Fuck off, said Dek. If you kent what went on at the college whiles, you'd ken I wasn't desperate.

Don't start in on that student shite again, Derek.

Hunter, just cause you're stuck in this hole seven days a week, doesn't mean you're getting any other kind of hole. The fucking opposite! Don't talk to me about desperate.

I won't talk to you about fuck all. . .

Here, cool it, cool it, broke in Bri, waving his hands in the air between us. Cool the fucking beans, lads. Me and Dek both picked up our glasses, suddenly remembered they were empty, and put them down again. Anyway, said Bri, wiggling his eyebrows, Some folk won't have to pay for it maybe.

Dek snorted and looked away. Dream on, he muttered.

The band finished a set of reels, and the announcement was made that stovies were being served in the small hall. Immediately a mob of folk formed round the door into the other room. Even the musicians laid down their instruments and jumped off the stage to join in the rammy. Above the shouts and laughter, the big singer could be heard crying, Let me through, I'm a fat bastard! as he elbowed his way to the front.

I stood up, rubbing my hands together. Well, who's for a plate of grease and tatties?

Bri mimed drinking a full pint. Liquid nourishment! he said, and wiped his mouth with the back of his hand.

I do fancy some stovies actually, said Dek. Soak up some of this alcohol, ken?

Fuck's sake man, I said, It's over late for that! You'd have to drain your whole blood supply into a bucket and dook in a sponge to soak up the booze in your body!

Least I've got some booze in my body, you fucking poofjuice, he said quietly, and stood up to face me.

Bri jumped up too. Aye, you've got a nerve you have, Hunter: showing up in public late and stone-cold sober! Call yourself Scottish?

What! Here's the boy who nicked half my pint when I did finally get my hands on one!

Ach, come on, said Dek. Let's stop yapping and go through. Paddy can stand his hand – afore he fucking disappears again.

Aye, a pint of stovies and a plate of lager for me, said Bri, and headed off, Dek after him. I checked my wallet, then followed them across the dancefloor.

It was scattered with ash and fag-dowps, and the polished wood was scuffed and marked with black sole-skids where folk had been dancing wildly and slipping about. In the middle of the floor Eddie the hallkeeper was standing with a tub of some whitish grainy dust. He'd dig his hand in, scoop out some of the dust, and cast it away towards the side of the hall; then he'd shift round a little and cast out some more. Half of the floor was covered with the stuff, and it made a crinching sound as folk walked across it from their seats to the small hall and back again.

What's this, Eddie? I said as the three of us passed him. Sow the seeds and scatter?

You scatter, you buggers, he replied, digging in his hand and lifting out a pile of the stuff.

We stopped.

It's to soak up the beer and the puke and that, eh Ed? said Bri.

Eddie gazed at the powder in his hand, watched a couple streams of it rickling out and down onto his shoes and the floor around his shoes. Any of you young buggers start puking and you're out of my hall before you can say Jock Robinson. He flung the dust away from him, scowling.

Come on, lads, said Dek, The queue's going down at the bar.

We were about to move off, when Eddie suddenly dropped to his hunkers with a moan. He started scraping at a blob of some sticky stringy stuff on the floorboards, eventually picking it off with his fingernail and dropping it in the pocket of his overalls. He stroked the polished wood with the flat of his hand, rubbed something invisible between his thumb and fingers, then looked up at us.

Slipperene, boys, this is the stuff! Can't have a dance without it!

God aye, they use it by the ton in Ritzy's in town, said Dek. Everybody raving away and the Ritzy jannie's going round with his bucket of Shitterene. . .

The three of us laughed. Eddie, standing up, didn't. He turned away and started chucking the stuff about as before, sighing: Slipperene, Slipperene. . .

Get your slippers and pipe out, it's the geriatric two-step! said Dek. He tottered off towards the other room, and Bri followed him. I hesitated.

What's it for, this stuff?

It's for the dancing. So you can get the slides in and that with the feet. Essential for a proper dance: a good seal and polish and a sprinkle of Slipperene half way through.

Get the feet flying, eh Eddie?

He moved me to one side with the back of his hand and aimed a fistful of stuff out over where I'd been standing. That's what it's all about, lad, getting the feet moving. With the real dancing, anyhow; I'm not talking about this modern rubbish where they just stand in one spot and jiggle up and down! There's been a bit of that thenight. He shook his head. I watch them doing it, jiggling up and down. . .

Hih, I bet you do.

Aye, and what's the use of dancing if you don't get anywhere?

That's what it's all about Eddie, no doubt at all. If only I could get somewhere sometime.

He looked at me for a moment from slits of eyes, then turned away. I better get on with this, he muttered, and was straight away engrossed again in casting out the Slipperene towards undusted patches of the floor.

When I got into the small hall, Dek was leaning against the wall by the window, arms folded. He nodded towards the bar set up on folding tables at one end of the room; Bri was standing there in the midst of a bunch of folk, shouting his order over the heads of the people in front of him. I shrugged a shoulder in his direction.

What's he up to Dek? I was going to get them.

Dek moved his feet. Ach, we didn't ken how long you'd be, newsing to Eddie there. Plus Bri has a right drouth on him – got a bit overheated with all that dancing maybe.

I shrugged both shoulders. Aye, fair enough, but no need to count me out of things, like. I mean I was just coming.

His eyes followed somebody walking behind me. How could we know? We thought you'd maybe abandoned us again.

Fuck's sake! I told Bri already about that earlier: I had to take some grub to my gran and granda. Just one of those things you have to do. I don't understand why you're so. . .worried about it.

He laughed to himself a wee bit, then looked at me as if I was some kind of a wee kid. Aye, you don't understand, that's the problem. Time was you would've understood straight off. Mind you, time was you wouldn't've needed to understand, cause you wouldn't've been letting your mates down in the first place.

Fuck's sake, Dek, I don't believe this. A year ago or something you wouldn't've been getting all worked up about this: me half an hour late or something cause I had to see the old folks? Blood's thicker than water, Dek, you ken that

63

He shook his head, looked beyond me again, then back. Fucking shite, Paddy. Beer's thicker than blood. If you get my drift.

I get your drift, I know where you're coming from, it's just. . .och, fuck it, Dek. It's getting to be a waste of time, this.

He smiled at someone over my shoulder, and raised a hand to wave. I whipped round, there was nobody there. Get to fuck, I said.

I turned and walked away from him, raging: inside I was raging. My head was filled with heat, hot blood, filled to bursting with burning blood thumping away at my brain. I closed my eyes and looked at the darkness there for a minute, looked into the dark, imagined it cool, imagined me falling down into it, out of the heat, into the darkness, into the cool – cooling my brain, cooling my blood, cooling me down altogether, for ever.

Well now, Patrick, how many?

I opened my eyes. I was right at the kitchen hatch in the end wall, and Mrs Duguid was leaning out of it, one eyebrow raised. Eh. . .

Oh, but I'll tell you what, we've just newly run out of plates. I'll have to give you it in these, okay?

She was holding a tall stack of polystyrene cups in one hand, the top ones weaving about in a circle as she moved her arms. For a second I couldn't work out what the hell she was talking about. Then she moved to one side, picked up a wooden spoon from somewhere, and plunged it into one of the enormous steel pots that were sitting on top of the big hall cooker. She moiled it round a couple times then dug in and hefted it out, a big scoop of dark brown stovies piled up on top. The stack of cups was swung over above the pot-mouth, and a flick of the wrist flipped ninety per cent of the stovies into the top cup, the rest falling back into the bubbling kirn in the pan. She leant through the hatch and thrust the cup in my direction. I took it, grease and gravy dribbling down the outsides of the cup onto my skin.

What are you looking like that for, loon? said Mrs Duguid. It's a good deal: you get more in a cup than on one of thon wee paper plates.

I stared at the cup for a second, then at her, then remembered what I was doing. You better give me another two, I said, Two for the lads, or else I'll be getting accused of starving them to death next!

She nodded and went back to the pot, pausing on the way to drink from a can of cider.

Dek seems in a bit of a funny mood thenight, Mrs Duguid, I said. I have the idea he's been in a funny mood the past couple times we've been out.

She grunted something, scooping up stovies.

What? I said. He's not taking sick or anything, is he?

She slid a cupful across the counter towards me and dug in her spoon again, said nothing.

He doesn't seem his usual self.

She stuck the spoon straight down in the middle of the pan, stood it upright in the thick mess, and moved over, dumping the last cup of stovies in front of me and looking me in the eye, frowning.

He was alright at teatime, last time I saw him.

Aye? Ah well. . .

But folk do change, Patrick, it can't be helped.

I looked at her. So you've noticed it as well, have you? Has he been acting funny at home? I mean I'm only asking cause he's my mate and that, I. . .

No, no, she broke in. Derek's fine. It's you I'm talking about.

Me? No, I'm not talking about me. What? Mrs Duguid, it's Dek we're talking about!

Well I've no time to talk about him, or anybody. She snatched up her can and took a drink. Now would you mind shifting away from the hatch?

But. . .

Come on, Patrick, move! There's folk wanting served.

The blood was starting to heat up in my brain again. I arranged the cups of stovies in a triangle on the counter and bent to pick them up like I was carrying three full pints, two in the crook of my thumbs and the other pressed in against them by my outstretched fingers.

I turned and walked back towards the middle of the room. There was nobody queuing for stovies, in fact there was hardly anyone left at all. Bri was served and gone from the bar, and Dek was away from where he'd been standing. It looked like the buggers were getting back at me by fucking off and leaving me alone. Someone rushed past me from behind, nudging my elbow and sending a splatter of stovies out of the cups and down onto the floor: it was Mrs Duguid heading for the bar. I stood on one foot, and lifted my other knee so I could balance the cups on it for a second and get a better grip. I didn't want to drop the lot halfway across the dancefloor, and have Eddie pissed off with me as well as everyone else.

The main hall was loud with the talk and laughter of folk sitting around the tables and along the walls, and there was the scraping of chairs and tablelegs as people moved them to get sat, back from the bar or the bogs. Up on stage, one of the band was tuning his guitar; if he did that after another hour or two's drinking, half the crowd would get up and dance to it. The Slipperene was skity and made a faint gritty noise under my feet as I crossed the dancefloor: it was like walking over a sheet of ice. I watched my step.

As I neared our table, my eyes on the stovie arrangement and the floor, somebody came bumping into me, gave a wee yelp, and said my name. I looked up; it was Shona the chef, still in her white jacket, but with her hair untied now and loosely hanging about her face.

Hello Paddy. . .sorry there!

Never mind, never mind. I looked down at my shoes: there were wee dauds of beef and tatties skittered on them and on Eddie's fine floor. Nothing serious, I said.

That's good. Who needs serious at this time of night? She smiled. I'll give you a hand. She took two of the cups and walked towards the table I pointed out.

I flicked each foot in turn to shake off the worst of the mess, and followed after her. What I want to know is, who makes these bloody stovies anyway? They're useless! Far too watery!

Shona put the cups down on the table. There was no sign of the lads, just one pint of heavy.

See stovies for a dance? I went on. They should be thick enough that you could dance a Strip the Willow with a plate in each hand and never spill a drop. None of this calfie's scour!

I sat down, and Shona did too, wiping her fingers on the underside of the table as she settled.

Say what you like, Paddy. I'm off duty as of ten minutes ago when I delivered the last tureen, so I don't give a shit what you say. There's Shona Findlay the chef, and Shona Findlay the human being, and they hate each other's guts.

I pulled the pint towards me, manouevering it through the

cups of tatties and gravy. I don't fancy that, I said. Sounds a bit confusing.

It is! Cause the human being keeps getting the chef into trouble by trying to make an appearance during working hours, and the chef keeps barging in during the human being's sociable hours, shagged out and bad fucking tempered!

I took a sip of my drink. Christ, I hope you didn't get pulled up for giving me those pies.

She shrugged. Ach, they probably won't be missed. I could say they were past their best or something, I suppose. Anyway, speaking as the human being, it's good to see the grub going to somebody who appreciates it for a change.

Aye, and they did: my granda thought it was great. Compliments to the chef! I mean, to the human being!

She grinned. You should see the amount of stuff that gets chucked out of there. But if they catch you taking home a bit of chicken or a slice of gateau, Wilson hits the roof. You have to stick it in the bin when somebody could be getting the good of it!

Well, thanks human, thanks chef. It was really nice of both of you. But here, let me get you a drink or something. I mean, I owe you. . .

Are you not with somebody?

I waved my hand at the empty space on the bench beside her. I'm on my own, Shona. As per always.

Ach well, all the more grub for you then. Where's your spoon?

Shit! I forgot to pick one up. I looked at the stovies in the three cups; it was starting to cool and congeal, a leathery-looking skin forming over each cup. To be honest Shona, no offence, but I don't really have the stomach for this any more. I mean I had my tea not that long ago, so. . . I was really just getting the stovies for the lads – Dek and Bri, ken? But this was their table, and now they've pissed off somewhere.

Maybe they're away to the bog, just.

But look: no pints! I ken they're boozy buggers, but I reckon they'd stop drinking long enough to have a jimmy riddle!

She laughed. There was a slight gap between her two front teeth. When she used to come and see my sister after school, I thought it made her look like a rabbit. Knowing me then, I probably even told her. But now there was something nice about it, something that made me want to hug her. But knowing me now, I probably wouldn't tell her this.

Maybe they have gone to the bog, she was saying. Maybe they've gone to pour their pints straight down the pan, save the trouble of actually drinking them.

Hih! Speaking of which, can I. . .

What? Ach, no Paddy, thanks but no. I mean I don't much these days. Plus I really only came in to drop off the stovies. I just washed the grease off my hands and was away home when you caught me.

Go on! Just one!

Nah, I'm driving, ken: I don't like to. Here! She stopped talking, grabbed my drinking wrist with one hand, and pointed with the other to the far side of the hall. That's a cosy wee confab!

After a second I made out the group of folk she was pointing at. Crowded around a single table down by the stage, as well as the blonde dame and the tall guy, were Dek and Bri, a couple other folk I didn't ken, and John Wilson from the Auld Mill. The tall guy was talking, moving his hands around in the air in front of him, like he was juggling with hot coals, and everybody else was looking on agog. Even Dek was grinning and nodding.

Who's that they're with? said Shona. They're not from around here, are they?

Brindle, they're called. From down south somwhere. Just moved up.

Aha! Brindle? They had a table for four thenight. Ordered lots of big à la carte stuff. Not much wonder Wilson's sucking up to them. Anybody that comes into the Mill and spends sixty quid on grub is his kind of folk.

I pushed my half-drunk heavy away towards the cups of cold stovies. Let's get out of here, Shona. I'm fed up of this fucking dump.

She looked surprised. Don't leave just cause I'm not staying.

Nah, I can't really be bothered biding here if my so-called mates are hanging about with the hoi polloi. I mean I can hardly go over and sit next to Wilson after earlier on, can I?

Not that you'd want to.

Right. And it's no fun on your own: you need a crowd to have a laugh. Or a couple just, a couple folk can have a great time together. But by yourself you just sit and fucking think about things.

Shona went to say something, but I kept coming up with reasons why I should leave with her.

Plus I'm too sober, that's another problem. I haven't drunk nearly enough to have a good time. This is fucking old Scotland after all. Imagine it, some bastard trying to have a good time without getting blootered! Impossible!

She shook her head, smiling, showing the gap between her teeth. You don't half go on, Paddy. The reason you don't get drunk is probably cause you blether too long inbetween swallows.

I lifted my glass again. Right enough, I said. Look at this pint, for instance; you wouldn't think I bought it more than three weeks ago and it's still not finished.

Are you going to finish it now?

From the stage came a loud burst of accordion, and

70

immediately whole tablefuls of folk rushed out onto the floor. The band wheeched into Crystal Chandeliers.

No, I said. Let's go.

As we reached the door out of the hall, I looked back. Bri was dancing with Mrs Brindle again. Marjorie to her friends. He caught sight of me leaving and took his hand off her arse to wave to me, signalling I should come back and join in the dance. I went on out.

The carpark was quiet and dark. We made our way between the lines of cars, past a couple of hired minibuses. Her white jacket seemed to be giving off a glow as it moved in front of me. Then she stopped, waited for me to catch up, and asked after Helen.

Christ, I said, Folk're always asking me how Helen is. Nobody ever asks how I am! It's typical of her. . .

Ha! I can see how you are, Paddy, I don't need to ask! If you were two hundred miles away and Hel was here I'd be asking her how you were. She walked on again.

Except you wouldn't, I said, striding to keep up with her.

Aye I would.

No you would not.

Would sut!

But you wouldn't, cause (a) I thought you'd fallen out with her about going away to college, and weren't talking at all. And (b) cause you're not interested in me, you're not a friend of mine, so why should you ask about me?

Ha! Oh aye. . . She laughed quietly to herself.

I sighed. That's the problem with this place: there's nobody who'd ask after me even if I was a million miles away.

She waved her hands in front of her. No, listen, I wasn't talking about that; I was minding on me and Helen falling out. God, that was years ago! I'd forgotten all about it.

Couldn't've been as big a row as it sounded coming up to my bedroom from the kitchen then.

Ach, we get on fine now. I mean we haven't met up recently, but we send postcards and stuff, and. . .here, you nebby bastard! Were you listening in to our private conversations? You bugger!

I had my fingers in my lugs and the radio turned up full blast, but you still came through loud and clear! I'll tell you, Shona, if you ever get fed up of this cheffing you should get my boss Murray to sign you up for the mart. Save money on the PA for livestock sales: just put you on, tell you to open up full thrapple.

She laughed. Here, I'm a mellow kind of person these days. Don't go around saying I'm loud.

Pardon? What? Sorry, I've gone temporarily deaf due to the force of your vocal cords. . .

Suddenly she flung out an arm, I thought she was going to clout me, instead she grabbed the lobe of my lug and gave it a yark. I yelled. She pulled me down towards her, at the same time standing on her tiptoes, bringing her lips up so they skiffed my skin along the cheekbone. . .then she jumped away.

We both stood frozen for a long second, then I turned to face her. Eh, Shona, was that a kiss?

What? You're joking? It was. . . I was just going to bawl in your. . .Patrick Hunter, dear oh dear! She shook her head, arms folded, half away from me. Then she looked back, gave a half-laugh. Okay, call it a kiss if you like. I don't mind.

I took a step towards her. I don't mind either. I reached out my hand towards her elbow.

Eh. . .hold on, she said.

That's what I was going to do.

She looked around the darkness of the carpark. No, but we're awfully out in the open here. She nodded to the lighted door of the hall thirty metres away. Fuck's sake, you never know who's going to come out of there.

And catch us talking? What an affront!

I could see her teeth white in the shadows of her face as she smiled. The gap would be there, but I couldn't make it out.

Nah, let's walk on to the car, she said. I mean we're going there anyway. We can talk as we walk.

Speak for yourself. That's stretching my brainpowers a bittie.

It's just, well, I do like talking to you, she said, as we moved on. I don't ken why. You're funny.

Christ, I'm glad somebody thinks so. Most folk round here just say I'm a pain in the neck.

I felt her looking at me. Most folk! I wouldn't say that. I always thought you were funny.

I. . .hih. Good. I shifted slightly so I was veering towards her as we walked out from the last of the cars.

The sounds of music and the yells and stomping from the hall were getting fainter, and we were walking down a slope, our feet crunching over gravel and sand. I stopped, looked at the dark line of trimmed trees on each side of us. Wait on, I said, This is the way to the graveyard.

Shona grabbed for the elbow of my jacket, tugged it, carried on walking. Come on, what are you feart of?

Eh. . .nothing. I went along beside her. Fearless I am, ready for anything!

Aye, very good: I saw you being fearless earlier on with John Wilson. Fearlessly making trouble for me!

Fuck, I'm sorry, I. . .here, is that why you're dragging me

73

down to this dark and lonely corner? Are you going to wreak your terrible revenge?

Nah, I'm parked down here, that's all. Would you believe it? Can't park Jan outside my work these days, in case Bobby Bastard comes along and takes out his flipping mental aggression on her bodywork.

Christ, you've not taken up with him again, have you?

No, that's the thing. I mean just cause I've moved back here he thinks I want to get back involved with him too. But we've only been seeing each other on and off. It was years ago I was *really* into him, when I was fifteen or sixteen or something. That doesn't count, I was just a kid. Now it's him that's acting like a kid. Week last Tuesday he let down all my tyres, can you fucking believe it? And he wonders why I won't move in with him!

We were approaching the big iron gates of the graveyard; they were black against the starriness of the sky beyond. Under a tree to the right of the gates I could see metal and glass glinting: Shona's 2CV.

So you're finished with him then?

It was after midnight, me just finished work. I had to pay for a taxi home!

Aye, I heard. But. . .

Tsh. I bet you did.

Well, you ken what this place is like.

Aye, that's one thing about being back, back in this place: some cunt causes a scene and five minutes later the whole fucking population knows about it. What an embarrassment!

I stopped walking. We'd reached the car. Shona carried on round to the driver's side, and felt in her pockets for the keys. The worst of it is, she said after a second, I suppose I still. . .well, I do still love him, ken? I mean that doesn't just disappear overnight.

74

But what's the point of being in love with a total arsehole? I don't know. But I am.

I came round the back of the car, passed her, and went up to the gates. I grabbed hold of them and pulled. They rattled but didn't move. I took a new grip on the cold twisted iron and yanked: no give at all, just the clanking of a chain. Behind me Shona said something.

They're locked! I cried. What's going on? The bloody graveyard gates are locked!

What's up?

I shook the gates with all my arms' strength. Open you bastards! Let me in! I'm wanting fucking in!

My voice and the sounds of the rattled metalwork trailed off into the night. I turned away and back to the car. Shona was sitting in the driver's seat with the door open and her feet on the ground. She was rolling a cigarette on her knee.

I can't get in, I said. Locking the gates of the bloody public cemy! Bastards!

She looked up, hair hanging in strands and loose curves down each side of her white face and onto the shoulders of her white jacket, more strands down in front of her eyes and mouth, getting in the way as she raised the makings to her lips to lick the gummed edge.

What're you wanting in for anyway? You drunk or something?

Christ, chance would be a fine thing! Two pints I've had. No, one! Cause Brian Milne had half the first one and I just left most of the second. Fucking Friday night, half past eleven and less than a pint down the hatch: disaster! Not much wonder I'm going to kill myself!

She flicked her head back, making the hair swing out of the

way long enough for her to put a lighter flame to her fag and get down the first lungful before it fell in front of her face again.

Get in the car, she said. If you've finished breaking into the graveyard, like. I'm needing home. Are you?

I nodded, made my way round to the passenger's side.

We drove off, slowly up the sandy graveyard drive, then faster once we got through the hall carpark and out onto the main street.

Here, I said after a minute, That cigarette smells funny.

Aye, said Shona, taking it from between her lips and holding it out to me. Do you want a blow?

Eh, no, no, not thenow. Christ, the car's that full of fumes all I need to do is breathe in!

She placed the rollie back between her lips and continued to smoke as we drove along through the square, past the end of Albert Street, and over the Shakkin Briggie.

After a period of silence, except for the lawnmowering engine of the 2CV, Shona muttered something.

What? I said.

She cleared her throat, and said, Witches do stuff in graveyards, eh?

Eh. . .I don't know.

They dig about to get nails from coffins, and bits of bones and stuff.

You're not thinking the gates of the cemy were locked against witches, are you? More likely the elders of the kirk trying to stop Gary Begbie from using it for illicit glue-sniffing!

Well, em. . . Can I tell you something, Paddy? I've never told anyone yet, I don't know who to tell. Helen, maybe, but she's not here, so. . . Ach, no, it's rubbish, forget it.

No, come on, Shona, I don't mind listening.

You won't believe me.

I will! I will believe you! Well, I'll listen, I promise that. Then I'll work out if I believe you. How's that?

I looked at her, but she was staring straight ahead. Her eyelids seemed to be drooping shut. How's that? I said again, loudly. Her eyelids flickered for a second, then they closed to slits again behind her hair, and she inhaled, waited, and breathed out, speaking.

It was a couple weeks ago, Paddy. A fortnight themorn, to be exact. Mind what that was?

Eh. . .a Saturday.

Aye, but it was the 31st: Halloween. And Wilson had kept me late in the kitchens yet again, cause the fucking dishwasher was on the blink, and me and wee Drew had to do everything by hand: plates, cutlery, glasses, pans, roasting trays – every-fuckingthing.

That's a bastard for a Saturday night.

Just about Sunday morning by the time we got finished! Midnight, anyway. Jesus! So I jump into Jan here, and I'm toddling along the Aberdeen road towards home, half asleep, right, but not been drinking or anything, and there's not a soul around. The streets are dead. Somebody letting their dog pish on the manse gate and that's it. But. . .are you listening?

Aye. I turned to watch her as she spoke.

I'd just passed the kirk, right, when something caught my eye, made me slow and stop, made me look again into the woods behind the kirk. There was a light there.

There's no houses there, it's just trees. . .

Aye, but there was a light in the middle of the trees, right in the Kirk Woods. There was a light burning: a fire.

A forest fire?

No, nothing like that. Just a bonfire, ken?

I frowned. I can't work that out.

Aye, but you've not heard the half of it yet. Listen: mind there's a kind of forestry track into the woods, half a mile or so on from the kirk?

The old drove road.

Whatever. The point is, there were cars parked in there, pulled well in off the road, right under the trees. I mean, I was looking for them – or something – otherwise I'd never've noticed them. And the gate at the end of the track was pulled shut after them. So what do I do? I stop Jan. Why? Cause I'm a crazy bitch with nose problems, right? Plus, it was beginning to seem like I was kind of meant to've been kept on late. . .

Well, Wilson did mean to, didn't he?

No, but like it was meant, a fate kind of thing, ken. Like the reason I was working late was just so that synchronistically I could pass and see these cars hidden in the woods, their engines still warm, and that noise coming out from amongst the trees.

My gaze had shifted away from Shona and out to the headlights flowing over the road and the verges and the trunks of trees. Now I snapped it back to her face. She wasn't smiling, she was staring straight ahead, concentrating on the driving, her lips working on the rollie of their own accord.

What sort of noise? I said.

It was a kind of a singing, but with a thumping in it as well: like a drum or something.

Eh, are you having me on? Midnight drumming in the Blackden woods? Nah!

78

She looked round sharply. I thought you were going to listen.

I'm listening! I am! Cross my heart. I traced a finger over the centre of my chest. It's just. . .weird, ken.

Aye, but like I said, you've not heard the half of it. She shifted gear as we started climbing the steep bit of road not far below The Strath. I walked on past the cars, going deeper into the woods. I was curious to see whatever it was that I'd been sent to see. And I did feel that I'd been sent, somehow, otherwise I wouldn't've been hanging about. I was just about crapping myself by this time! But I kept on for five minutes or so, along the track to start with, and then right into the trees, all the time the firelight getting closer and the voices getting louder. And it wasn't singing, more of a kind of chanting, and maybe not a drum, maybe just feet thumping on the ground as they danced around the bonfire.

Fuck's sake!

Aye, fuck's sake.

Could you see who it was?

Aye, I went up and shook their hands!

What!

Paddy. . . She looked at me, eyebrows raised behind her fringe, then took out her fag and flicked it away through the flap of her window. I was just about feart for my life, she went on. Feart that they'd smell me out or something, sense I was there and come after me and catch me and. . .I don't know what. So I was just creeping up, always on the point of turning and running, trying to be as quiet as I could. Then I got about twenty metres away: that was close enough, close enough to see.

To see what?

Half a dozen folk, women and a man, dancing round the fire in the nuddy, in front of this big kind of altar stone. . .

What! You're joking?

Do I look like I'm FUCKING JESUS! She slammed on the brakes.

WHAT? I had my seatbelt undone and my hand on the door, ready to run.

Christ! She looked over her shoulder, reversed the car quickly back the way we'd come, then screeched it to a halt. Just about missed your turning, she said, nodding beyond me. My house was sitting there, dark at the end of its dark track. How many times have I come up here? Thousands! But not for a while, I suppose.

I was listening too hard to your story, I. . .

Paddy! She took her hand off the wheel and raised a finger, stared into my eyes and drew a straight line between us with it, from her to me and back again. This is not a story. This is the truth.

So you really. . .

Aye. I really saw what I'm telling you now. And the reason I'm telling you is cause I thought you'd believe me. She looked at me. I thought you'd trust me that it was real.

I do. I do believe you, actually. I nodded, then shook my head. I mean, you read in the papers about Satanic stuff, Babies Sacrificed in the North-East and that, but. . .

Get a grip! This was nothing like that. Alright, it was midnight. Alright, they were dancing round a bonfire in the woods. Alright, they were starkers. But there was nothing strange going on, nothing nasty. Nothing suspicious roasting on the fire, or bleeding on the altar, nothing like that at all.

What was it then, the Womens' Guild social night?

It wasn't evil, but it wasn't boring either. It looked more kind of exciting, kind of as if they were in touch with the really old powers. Ken, the ones the rest of us have forgotten about? I mean, I won't kid you, I was shitting myself, but I was also kind of

thinking, God, I wish I could find out what all this is about. . .
Cause I bet they've got a lot of wisdom, Paddy, a lot of answers for
the world's problems.

They sound a bit like my auntie's political chums, I wanted to say,
but I didn't think Shona would see the similarity. Instead I said, Hey,
now you mention it, there was that lassie up at Crathie – Davidson,
Janet Davidson was it? – they used to say she was a witch.

Shona gave the steering wheel a little bang with her hands.
Ach, old folk just said that cause she used to sleep around a bit.
With the squaddies from the Balmoral guardhouse. This isn't like
that.

Do you want to come in for a cup of coffee or something? She
didn't reply, just gazed out into the dark. No, just with it getting a
bittie cold sitting here.

Well. . .

You could come in and get heated up a bit.

Aye, but no. I'll tell you, no. I should just be getting home, I'm
pretty shagged out and that. She yawned all of a sudden.

Oh. That's a pity. Well, thanks for. . .but listen: you haven't
told me the end yet. I mean, did they find you? What were they
singing about? Did they, like, do anything else?

Shona got the makings out of her jacket pocket, rolled another
skinny cigarette and got it going, all without speaking, except for
a few wee grunts of concentration.

It was hard to make out, she said after a few puffs. But it was
something about: I am the light and you are the dark, I am the
dark and you are the light, blah blah blah, open your arms and
embrace it, blah blah blah. And they kept repeating the bit about I
am this and you are that. . .

I thought for a second, but it came to nothing. So what did you
do? I said.

I just basically went home. And the next day I woke up and for a minute I thought I'd dreamed the whole thing. But no, there was mud on my jacket, and grass stains on my jeans. And I felt like I wanted to tell somebody about it, or ask somebody what they thought, but who could I tell? Not Bobby Bastard, for starters, he'd just take the piss. Not my folks. Helen maybe if she was here. I didn't really think of you, Paddy, till we were talking thenight. Suddenly you seemed like the ideal person to tell. She took a deep draw on the fag, and sighed as she exhaled.

I don't ken what to say, though. I mean I've not been much use. It's so hard to get a handle on, ken? I blinked; my eyes were nipping with the thickness of the smoke in the car. I know there were witches here hundreds of years ago, I said. Back in fifteen-oatcakes Blackden was famous for them. The only thing it's ever been famous for! We did them in school, and my granda's told me about them too. But this is fucking. . .it makes my head birl! And my heart, it's going like, I don't know, like a fucking sink plunger! I'm all mixed up here! I mean, naked witches dancing round a fire in the Kirk Woods? It's just. . . Do you want to come in for. . .?

She blew out a big puff of smoke. I coughed.

I'm heading home now, she said. You better get out.

Aye. . .eh, aye. I opened the car door a little. A blast of cold air came in and hit me on the side of the face; the other cheek felt like it was burning hot all of a sudden. Well, I said, Thanks for the lift and for telling me the. . .well, I don't know.

I shrugged, got out of the car, and stood there, noticing for the first time that we'd stopped right in the middle of the road. Shona shouted something after me. I opened the door wide again, and leant in towards her.

I'll see you themorn, she said.

Oh aye, sure, I said. Where?

The party at Bunce's, late on. Eh. . .I thought you'd ken.

Bunce Coban's?

Aye.

Grand, I'll see you there then!

Well. . .

And if you turn into a frog before then, come along to me, I'll kiss you better!

What?

If the witches put a spell on you, ken.

Oh aye. . .well. She started the engine and looked out the front. I ken where to come then, she said.

Aye, I wish you would come, cause my ma's away for the weekend, and. . .

Goodnight, she said, pulled the door shut, and drove off.

I stood there, feeling dizzy or lost or reisted, like something had wandered inside me. The lights of the car disappeared, and the noise of its engine too. All around was quiet and darkness, except for the yellow glare of the Blackden streetlamps a couple miles down the road. They hurt my nippy eyes, I wished I could turn them out. Instead, I turned my back on them, and went in to bed.

Saturday

I biked along the denside road. The morning was clear and cold as the night had been, as all the past week had been. Sweat I'd worked up cranking through the village was turning to ice-water on my forehead. I'd've seen my breath hanging in the air, if I hadn't been speeding along and leaving it behind. Quite likely I was trailing clouds of the stuff out back as I biked, like the big jets that pass high overhead here heading for the North Pole and America. The vapour-trails they plough through the sky hang around for half an hour sometimes – white furrows in a huge blue field, too high for the gulls to follow. And then the straight lines shift and blur, and you're left staring up at nothing.

I pedalled on. Up the braeside, ahead and away to the right, there was a glinting that would be the windows of Goodman's Croft catching the low sun, and all inbetween the line of the road and the croft the parks were flecked with dazzlement where the frozen dew was bouncing back sunlight. The black of the road was silver with sprays of ice as well, odd puddles at the verge caked solid white.

Engine noise ahead made me look up. A couple fences away a tractor was bumping over the rough broken-up earth of a muckle park, bogey rattling along behind it. Halfway along the road side of the field it stopped, the engine cut, and somebody jumped down, immediately walking away from the tractor, eyes on the ground. He stopped, turned, and went back the way he'd come, then bent to pick something up from the earth, and chucked it into the cart. It clattered. He took another pace, chucked something else in, then carried on walking.

Before I reached level with the tractor, I'd recognised the guy as somebody who'd been in the year above me at the school, Roosty Ronaldson. The mannie Ronaldson did rent two three parks this side of the village, though his own farm was a couple miles north of it: Howbrae, up in the hills. I steered my bike over the road, swung off it, and propped it against the dyke. Roosty was nowhere in sight. A flat through-stone was sticking out halfway up the wall; I jockeyed myself up on that and went in over. Roosty stood up behind the bogey, heaved something over the side-board, and dropped it in. It thudded. Then he saw me, and leant on his elbows.

Aye aye, he said. Real heavy bugger that one!

What's this? Missed neeps?

Christ no: bloody stones just. Anyway, it was tatties in here, not neeps. He took off his John Deere baseball cap and scratched at his skull through a hussock of orange hair. Fucking stones caaed off half the tines on the lifter, couple weeks syne.

Rocky ground is it?

Reckon old Dod hadn't been over it for twenty fucking year: hell of a rummlie. He put his cap back on, peak pointing up at the clear sky.

This one of Dod's parks was it? I didn't ken.

Haw! I reckon he'd forgot about it himself this past while!

We looked over the rough earth. I'm away to Goodman's now, I said. The roup's theday.

85

Roosty nodded. Aye. Daresay I'll look in by. The old man's going up, I ken that. Reckon he's after something.

If it's junk he wants he'll be okay. I laughed. Biggest hillock of rusty shite I've ever worked with!

He nodded again. Ah well. We'll see. Here, he said after a second, You can give me a hand with this one bastard of a thing. He walked off across the patch of ground he'd been clearing.

I hesitated, then followed him. I've got to get to my work really. I just thought I'd say hello when I saw you, ken? I mean I can't hang about.

Ach, don't fash yourself: this'll not take two minutes. He stopped walking and looked down. The stone at his feet, with the earth kicked away from the sides of it, must've been a metre long and nearly as wide.

We'll never shift that, I said.

Aye will we. You watch. He cupped his hands, spat into the hollow, and rubbed them together. You get that end, he said, and worked his fingers under the edges of the brute.

It was a big lump of dark grey granite, with two bright scars of silver where something metal had dragged across it. I put my hands to the sides and tried to get them under for a grip, but couldn't: the stone was over deep at my end, there was no sign of it flattening out.

Hold on, I said, and scrabbled away some loose earth from each side. The soil was cold, and I could feel it pushing under my fingernails, damp and gritty, as I dug deeper. Halfway to my elbows it was still stone going straight down. I don't ken about your bit, I said, But this goes down half a fucking mile.

He looked down at my end, then back at his. Tell you what, I'll kind of shoogle the point here up and down and that'll maybe loosen the bastard a bittie. We'll maybe coup her up and get hold of her that way.

He straightened up, stretching his back, then bent over, gripped the stone, and strained to raise it a fraction; he let his weight fall down on it, then yarked at it again, then next time I shoved down on it too; I let him lift it, then we both shoved down, and he lifted again. . . But even now it was only just trembling at his end, and my end not even that.

Roosty stood up, peching, whipped off his cap and wiped his wrist across the sweat on his forehead. Fuck-a-doodle-do! he said. This bastard's got hell of a deep roots!

I checked my watch. Look, Roosty, I'm going to have to be getting up to Goodman's, or the Murrays'll go daft. I'd like to muck in, ken, but work comes afore pleasure and that.

He waved the cap in front of his face. No bother, Paddy. I reckon I'll have to get the digger onto the bugger. Christ, five minutes in the park and defeated already! Bad news! He shook his head, and we walked towards the tractor, empty-handed. You have to keep on top of these stones, see – like old Dod fucking didn't – have to give them the fucking once over every year at least, clear them away, otherwise the bastards just sprout up all over the shop!

Worse than weeds, eh?

Aye, and they keep on coming, that's the cunt of it. He picked up a fist-sized rock and chucked it in over. Every year more appear. Where do they come from, the centre of the fucking planet? Christ, if they keep on at this rate the bastarding earth'll be hollow in a puckle years, all the stones'll be piled up in heaps and dykes on the surface. What then, eh? What fucking then? He banged the flat of his hand against the side-board of the bogey. All that weight up here and hollow down below: bad news! The earth'll never fucking stand it! She'll just caa in!

*

I'd stuck my bike away up the back of the cart-shed and was coming out the doors when the blue Murray Marts van pulled into the court of Goodman's Croft. I raised an arm in greeting.

Fine morning, said Sandra Murray, getting out of the driver's side and striding away towards the house, cash-box in one hand and catering pack of teabags in the other.

Just grand, I replied. It's days like this that make you think. . .

What? she said, as she paused to unlock the back door.

Eh. . .I don't know. Just think, maybe. Or maybe days like this make you think: I like days like this!

You been hitting the bottle before breakfast again, laddie? Dear oh dear. She disappeared inside the house.

Having spent a minute or two straightening his bunnet in the rear-view mirror, Bill Murray swung his beer belly out of the passenger's side and followed it round to the back doors of the van. What's this about beer for breakfast, Paddy?

Nah, nothing. Just me saying I'm raring to go, like. Don't worry.

He pulled his kist out of the van and held it under one arm till he'd closed the doors again. Ach, I'm not worried, loon: I ken what it's like. Sandra wouldn't understand, but I do. Hair of the dog, best thing for it sometimes. He squinted over the roof of the van at me. I've been there myself, Paddy.

I shrugged. I don't know, Bill: you run out of milk in the morning, what else can you do but put Highland Park on your cornflakes?

What? He was looking worried now.

Hih! Only joking, Bill, just pulling your leg!

God, I should think so: that dear malts is for special occasions, just. Stick to 100 Pipers or something for first thing in the morning, or it could get to be a dangerous habit.

For your health?

Nah, for your wallet!

Oh aye, hih. Good job you pay so well then, eh?

Bill didn't reply at first. He was looking at the buildings around the court, stroking the smooth-trodden wood of the kist with his free hand, thinking.

You work well, he said at last, not looking at me. So, eh, take this. He held out the kist towards me.

I thought for a second he was taking the piss and was going to snatch it away when I reached for it, but I reached for it and he didn't snatch it away and I had it in my hands. The first time in six months of work with the Murrays that I'd got hold of the kist.

Put that in the press in the kitchen, he said. After that come along to the bothy park. He'd clasped his hands in front of his belly like he was shaking on something with himself, and with the two of them joined in a clump indicated a gate into a field at the far end of the steadings. I took all the implements along there yesterday, he said, And I'll away now and line them up. I was that hashed at the time I just uncoupled them any old way. Then you come along and get them numbered and that. But I'll get them in proper straight dreels first. Otherwise folk would start casting clods at us, see?

Eh, aye. I got a good hold on the kist. It was heavy for its size, it felt more the weight of lead than wood. I'll get going then. I slowly turned away from Bill, and started towards the house. I looked back as I reached the door: he was standing by the van still, still looking around a bit, his eyes going from one bit of the court to another, then out past the byre and down the length of the track to the road. He looked like he was watching something, but there was nothing there yet. I went inside.

Sandra was at the scullery table, ripping open long packets of plastic cups and shaking them out onto a spread of beer and whisky trays. She looked up as I came in, her eyes flicking immediately to the kist.

My God, Paddy! What's happened?

Eh. . .nothing. I went round the other side of the table from her.

You walk in with Bill Murray's magic box in your hands and say that nothing's happened? He'll be wandering about like a headless chicken out there, like a kid without its cloot to suck!

I opened the door of the press and slid the kist to the back corner of it, next to a mousetrap that had something small and furry caught in it: either a mouse-corpse or a very mouldy bit of cheese. I gave the kist a wee tap with my toe, then shut the press door behind me again.

I suppose Bill's just coming to trust me or something. I mean about time too.

Nah, Paddy, there's something in the air theday. She shook her head, concentrating on righting all the plastic cups and arranging them in neat rows across the trays. You said it yourself, she went on, You were feeling happy or something this morning. Now what's behind that? I mean there must be something going about that's making you feel like that, and making Bill let the orra loon cart his precious kist about! It's not natural, that kind of behaviour. Happiness, that's something for special occasions, weddings and that, not just for everyday.

I went to go outside again. It's funny you saying that, Sandra, cause Bill was saying the same thing just a second ago.

We're not agreeing on something are we? Glory be!

Well, it was whisky he was talking about. . .

Ach!

. . .but I think that's why he gave me the kist too, cause I told him I had whisky for my breakfast. He thinks we've got something in common now. I reached for the door-handle.

He'd like to have something in common with you, she said. I think he looks at you and imagines. . .

Imagines what?

That if we had. . .ach, forget it. She turned away, then instantly back again, a fierce glower on her face. Get away from that door!

Eh?

Get the trestle table set up outside the front of the house there. And fill up the urn and plug it in at the porch. And after that get these trays out, and the teapots. And I'll've done the biscuits by then and they can go out and after that the real work starts: take all the stuff lying about in the larder there, all the pans and plates, any tins of food even, get them all out on the table here, or the floor too, get them all into decent lots – cause you never got round to that yesterday, did you?

Well, I did the rest of the house, but. . .

There's no time to talk, loon. Folk'll be arriving soon and we've got to be ready! Get to it!

But Bill said I was to go along. . .

. . .to the implements? Aye aye. And get them into nice straight lines, no doubt? The man's a dreamer! No one'll even look at that park till this afternoon, but they'll all be here in half an hour wanting their tea, you'll see. So get brewing!

I got.

By quarter to ten the grass park in front of the steadings was half full of cars and Land-Rovers and pickups. It looked like most of the farm folk for ten miles around had showed up, though you wouldn't've expected it, what with it being just a small croft roup, and not a well-equipped croft at that. I was saying this to Sandra while I waited for my cup of tea to cool down. Bill had given me the nod to have one when I told him I'd finished with the lots in the house, Sandra already having given me the nod to get the nod from Bill. For the next two or three hours we'd be too busy to have a break at all, but for now there was a wee while to spare. Sandra always gets into a bit of a working frenzy an hour or two before the start of a roup or a mart, so we're usually ready to go early, though sweating. Then she starts to calm down. She was pretty calm now, standing with her arms folded in front of her and looking down at the folk streaming out of the park and up to the court, and thinking up the usual kind of Sandra Murray reply to any question.

The country's got a dose of buying fever, that's what it is. She said it as definitely as if she'd just heard it announced on Radio Aberdeen.

I wish the weather was a bit more fevery, I said, cupping my hands around my tea and shivering.

Hm, well. No connection, Paddy, no connection there. It's a kind of craziness that comes across folk sometimes: I've seen it afore. Some empty space opens up in their head, and they try and fill it up by buying things. It doesn't matter what they buy so much, it's just the actual buying that's important.

I blew over the top of my cup to cool the tea, tried a sup, then waited some more. How does that urn do it? I said. I thought boiling was as hot as water could get. But this is hotter than that. It's like brown steam! I'll not get drinking it afore Bill wants to start the selling!

You see folk at the mart sometimes; they're buying beasts or sheep I *ken* they haven't got pasture for. Or at some displenish sale

92

like theday, there'll be one lot that nobody's going to buy, like a teachest of jelly-jars, and somebody eventually puts in a bid for fifty p, then somebody else a pound, till afore you know it the whole load's been knocked down to some old mannie with a mad look in his een and chicken shite on his boots.

I laughed. And you ask yourself, What the hell's he going to do with all thon jars?

Sandra tucked her chin into her neckfat, pursed her lips, and nodded. Behind her in the porch, the urn-lid started rattling, and there was a hissing and spitting as clouds of water escaped from inside.

It's like a fire-breathing dragon, that thing, I said.

Nah, I'm the only dragon about here, she said, and laughed. I laughed too. Aye, she said, I see you don't deny it!

Well. . .

Too late! Laughing more, she stepped through the open door of the porch and bent to adjust the controls on the urn.

A couple of farmers shauchled up to the table beside me: the Hendersons, elderly batchelor brothers from Waulkmill. Their eyes shifted across the pots and milk and sugar to Sandra in the porch.

Any chance of a cup of char? said one of them, the elder of the two. He was known as Geronimo.

Aye, any chance of a cup of char? said the other one. His name was Tonto, cause he was always the sidekick. They'd both had Indian names since I was a wee kid, probably because their surname had always been shortened to Hendoo, same as everybody else called Henderson, and the sound of the nickname reminded us of that folk in India, the Hindus. And what with these brothers' faces being all drunk red and burnt brown, that just about convinced us that they were Indians. And the only kind of Indians we kent about were the ones on the telly, the branch of them that had flitted over to America after the cowboys. And that's where we got their names from, and we used to shout after them if we saw them in the village, and go into a kind of war dance after they'd passed.

Who's in charge of the char? said Geronimo.

What is it, help yourself? said Tonto. There was no sign of a reply from Sandra.

I'll get it, I said, and nipped round the back of the counter. I poured two cups of strong black tea from the big tin teapot, then shoved them across the table, nodding at the bag of sugar and bottle of milk just in front of them.

How much, loon? said Geronimo.

Ten pence each. I pointed to a paper plate already scattered with ten and twenty pences.

And how much for the sugar? said Tonto.

The sugar? Well, nothing, on the house!

The sugar's free, said Geronimo, reaching out and starting to spoon the stuff into his cup. After five or six loads he stirred and stuck the wet spoon back in the bag. His brother immediately took it out and gave himself five or six spoonfuls too. Before returning the spoon to the bag he licked it clean. The two of them gave me thin smiles, put a pile of coppers each on the paper plate, and sclaffed off across the court. Sandra came up beside me.

That was the Hendersons from Waulkmill, I said.

Aye, I ken. Why do you think I was taking so long with the urn? They give me the creeps, those guys: they're like Tweedledee and Tweedledon.

Hey, Sandra.

What?

Do you take sugar in your tea?

No, I gave it up years ago. Why?

Oh, just wondered. I went back round the other side of the table, and picked up my cup. It was almost cold now, but still steaming: the air was that chilly.

I've been thinking about it, Paddy, said Sandra, And I have an idea what it is maybe.

What what is?

This buying fever.

You're not still. . .

No, but listen, I like to work these things out, get them right. And what it is, is, it's all these European subsidies. When we were lassies up on our father's place at Alford, we kent what was what: you planted tatties, and then you picked tatties, then you sold them. And you kent that not far away somebody was having them for their tea. But now what happens? You're about to get your planting done when a mannie from Europe comes along. Stop! he says. We've over much tatties this year: set-aside! So you've not to touch the park for another twelve month, but you get a fine big cheque from Brussels or somewye for doing bugger all! Money for nothing! It'd drive you clean gyte!

Hih. And then you'd come to roups and marts and spend the money you got for nothing on things you don't need. . .

As I was speaking, Bill Murray emerged from a group of men standing at the corner of the house and strode over to the table beside me. From dead slow and stop first thing, he'd worked up to a fair old speed of movement. By the time the bidding started he'd be pelting about like a peerie.

Aye, Bill, I said as he approached. Me and Sandra were just saying how folk've gone daft for spending their siller this past while.

Good for business, said Bill. Hope they keep it up. He crossed his fingers, then tapped them on the wooden top of the trestle table.

But you do feel sorry for the old folks, whiles, said Sandra, reaching out with a cloth and wiping the bit of table that Bill had tapped a second before. I mean, being rushed into selling their house or their gear, just cause some other body's putting up crackpot prices.

I nodded, drank the last of my tea. That's true as well. What did this place go for? Eighty thousand?

Free choice! said Bill. Nobody's forcing them to buy. If daft sassenachs want to throw their money away on... Suddenly he stopped, slowly turned his head to look over his shoulder, then slowly, slowly brought it back towards us again. Shh! he whispered.

What's up? I whispered back.

Careless talk costs profits, he said quietly, then suddenly burst into a louder than normal voice: Aye, so let's get yoked then. Where's my kist, loon?

In the kitchen press, Bill, where you told me to...

Fine!

Do you want me to go and...

God no, loon! Who do you think you are? He nodded at Sandra, then at me, as if we were acquaintances passing in the street, then turned and walked off quickly into the crowds.

We watched him go for a second, then Sandra stretched over to take the empty cup from my hand.

Ken this, I said. I mean, don't laugh, Sandra, but I'm almost feart sometimes when Bill starts getting like that, all sharp and stuff.

Hm well! That's not Bill! Well, it's half Bill, Bill halfway changed into Murray the Auctioneer. Him up on his kist talking away ten to the dozen: that's the one that's not Bill. And mind on this, Paddy, he was a roadman for the council when I met him, we were married seven year afore I ever saw that side of him. Now, that *was* a shock!

The noise of shouting and laughing and boots on cobbles suddenly died away to almost nothing. The folk hanging round the court and the various outbuildings were all starting to gather thegether in one particular place, looking in one particular direction, at the spot where Murray the Auctioneer was setting down his kist and getting his papers in order.

I bet it was a shock to him as well, I said, turning back to Sandra. It would be to me, anyroad: going along happily for years on end thinking you're one thing, then suddenly finding that. . .

You'd better get over there, Paddy, or you won't be going along anywhere: he'll have your guts for galluses.

Bill got the roup underway. The old Fordson tractor had been taken out of its shed the day afore and was lined up with Dod's bluntworn plough and other implements in the stubble park at the far end of the steadings. Now the floor of the tractor-shed had three dreels of sale items arranged up and down it: a hosepipe and stirrup-pump; a wooden plunge-kirn, its staves dried out and loosened; a roll of barbed wire; a set of riddles; a rusty neep-hasher. . . The shed looked like the rejects room at a museum of agriculture.

Bill had set down his kist just outside the door, and the folk were gathered inby, leaving a clear space immediately in front of him: this was my stamping ground. Murray would call out a lot, reading off the inventory on his clipboard – Alright gents, number fiftytwo, half a hundredweight of rat poison! – and I'd have to dive into the shed, check the numbers chalked on the concrete floor in front of each item, then heft up the foosty sack in question and go running outside with it. As I strolled around the ring, necks would start raxing, heads bobbing about, and I'd hoist the sack up onto my shoulder so that folk at the back of the steer could see what they were bidding for.

And all the time Murray would be standing over me, spitting out the running prices like a shotgun spraying pellets, his head wagging back and forth scanning the crowd for winks and nods and fingers tugging lugs, his tub of a gut bouncing up and down as he jigged about to the rhythm of his patter: One bid one bid I'm bid one surely two surely two one-fifty on my right one-fifty, two two two bid, two-fifty three four five six six at six bid six bid I'm bid six at the back at the back seven bid seven bid eight bid nine I'm bid nine nine, against you at the back, it's nine I'm bid surely make it ten now, ten? ten? at the back ten at the back ten bid going at ten now, all in at ten? ten, ten, hammer's up at ten. . . Thankyou!

He'd kick his heel down on the lid of the kist, the hollow thud marking the closing of the sale.

By this time I'd've nipped back into the tractor-shed, dumped the lot in its proper place, and emerged again to stand just behind Bill. As voices murmured briefly in comment on the price reached and the wisdom or naewiseness of the buyer, he'd hand me down a cloakroom ticket with the lot's number on it and the final price scribbled by him on the back. I had to've noticed who got the bid, and now shove through the crowd till I'd found them and given them the ticket. Then it was back into the shed again, listening out for the next number Bill announced, running up and down the lines of junk till I'd found it, then wandering about the ring with it held high.

Any unsold items weren't returned to the shed, but got carted off by me and dumped in a corner of the court to be sorted out later.

Fifteen minutes of this and the sweat was flying off me, the muscles in my back and legs and arms screeving with the strain of the bending and lifting and running. But there were a great number of lots at Goodman's, more than two hundred different items in the main session, and half of those had two or three parts to them: a worn-out besom and a hard-bristle byre-brush, a hundred metres of orange binder-twine and a sackful of odd ropes and tow; a scythe, a straik and a sickle. . . These composite lots were harder for me to bear about, but easier for Bill to sell. Folk'll turn up their noses at a, b and c one after the other, but if you stick them all in an old tattie-bag and throw in a useless lump of x and a broken y or z, they'll be fighting with each other to pay over the odds for the whole jingbang.

The roup went on.

I was hip-grippit. My muscles were aching, my lungs were knocking against my ribs, my brain was leaping about from lots to numbers to tickets to faces in the crowd, and my feet were tearing in and out of the shed, round and round the ring, up to Bill and away, out to the junk pile in the corner and back to the shed again. And after we'd emptied the tractor-shed we went straight on without pausing to the byre, Bill just lifting up his kist, walking along a few metres to outside the byre-door and setting up there as before, the steer shuffling along at his heels, arranging themselves in their circle around him, and me caught up in them, ducking elbows and tripping over muckle sharny boots to get to the front and alongside Bill then into the byre to find the first lot being sold: six steel milk churns. I took one of them out just, trundling it along at an angle, the noise of it bashing and clanging over the cobbles of the court so loud that I had to stand still for once or else I'd've drowned out Bill's patter completely. The churns were bought by the woman of the couple who run a goat-farm and cheese-makers over by Kincardine O'Corse. The next lot was a couple of wee milk-flagons I'd found hanging from the rafters of the cart-shed. The goat woman was eyeing them up, and Bill was just getting into his rhythm, when there was a roaring engine noise, and the sound of stones banging off the underside of a car as it sped up the rough track to the croft. A second later a big green Volvo shot round the corner and braked to a sudden halt, dirt showering, a metre short of mowing down the outer edges of the crowd of bidders.

Where's the fire? somebody said, and everybody else muttered and moaned, like a bingo hall disturbed halfway through a house. Bill stopped in mid-flow, his mouth open, one hand raised in the air, his belly still quivering. Apart from that, nobody was moving, except for a few who bent their heads to try and see into the car, to check who was crashing the roup. Whoever it was blasted their horn, one long parp, and it echoed loudly round the court. Folk grummled louder, and a few were scowling now and jerking their thumbs at the driver to clear off out of it.

Suddenly Bill unfroze and started waving his hands about in front of him. Wheesht, wheesht! he said. That's Mr Brindle, folks. Hold your wheesht now, he owns the place, he can drive up here if he likes. He was going red in the face.

He was just about over my foot! somebody cried. Wild bugger!

Now then, now then, shift out of his way, Bill said. He lifted his bunnet to the man in the car and gave him a sappy grin. The

Volvo's engine revved, and it began to move forward again; folk in its path shifted, slowly. Let him through, let him through, said Bill, waving people away with one hand and signalling for the car to drive on with the other.

You're in the wrong job, Murray, somebody said from the depths of the crowd. You should be in the middle of Union Street directing traffic!

Everybody laughed, and Bill did too, after his eyes had followed the Volvo out the other side of the crowd and seen it park at the far end of the court, close to the back of the house.

Bill shook his shoulders, cleared his throat, then gave the kist a few dunts with his heel till everyone had turned to face him again. Back to business, he said. There's still a heap of stuff to get through. Lot 185! I held the milk-flagons above my head and Bill launched in: Let's start at five then five pounds five pounds, four four, three surely three, two-fifty yes I'm bid two-fifty I'm bid three bid three bid three-fifty. . .

Sorry about that! A loud voice called out from the back of the crowd, and Bill froze again, his face gowping. A very tall man in a green waxed jacket and a flat tweed cap strode through towards the front. Sorry I'm late, Mr Murray, said Brindle.

It's not the kirk, somebody said from the crowd.

Brindle paid no notice. Damned nuisance, but unavoidable, he went on. Got caught up in a little contretemps with the manager of the hotel in Blackden! The steer had parted to let him get to the front, folk almost shrinking back as he passed them. Still, better late than never, eh! Eh? He stood inside the ring, and beamed round at the circle of bidders. Only Bill was the same height as the guy, and that was because he was standing on his foot-high kist. Brindle reached out and grabbed Bill's hand, frozen in mid-air in front of him, and wrung it.

Good to see you again, Mr Murray! All going well, I trust?

Eh. . .aye. I mean yes, Mr Brindle. Everything's going fine.

Brindle frowned. Fine? Just fine? Is something the matter then?

What? Eh. . .no, no, I mean fine as in, eh, grand. Everything's going grand.

Brindle nodded. Very good, very good. Well! Ha! I'd hoped to be here for the off, but I've evidently missed it. Never mind, never mind. Maybe I'll get a cup of something hot and sweet from your lady wife, and then I'll be back, back to the fray, eh! Eh? I'd love to catch a flavour of you in action, Mr Murray: wonderful old trade you practise!

Eh. . .

Carry on, carry on. Don't mind me.

He went to stride away again, but then stopped when he caught sight of me, still standing in the ring with the two flagons resting on my shoulders. He pursed his lips and looked up and down at me and the cans.

Aquarius! he said. The water carrier! No? Ha!

They're for milk, I said. Not water really.

Ah, very good, for milk.

Aye, they're for taking milk out of one thing and putting it into something else, Bill said from up on his box.

Like taking it out of a cow and putting it into your coffee perhaps, eh? Ha! Excellent. They're very handsome. I'll bid twenty pounds for the pair. Twenty pounds, Mr Murray!

Somewhere behind me the goat-woman said, Shit. . .

Eh. . .any more bids? said Bill.

Not at that price, somebody said quietly.

Well, sold to Mr Brindle then, said Bill, and let his foot fall on the kist with a sound like a clod of earth hitting a coffin lid.

Excellent, excellent, cried Brindle. Always happy to join in the spirit of things! Have them brought round to the kitchen later, eh?

Nodding left and right at the folk parting to let him through, Brindle passed through the crowd and headed off towards the house. Talking and coughing started to rise up out of the silence, and a few laughs too.

Now then, now then, said Bill. Let's get on with it.

Aye, let's get a flavour of your wonderful old trade, somebody said from the crowd, and Bill had to wait for the laughing to die down before he could continue selling.

An hour later Bill announced a fortyfive minute break and stepped down. He picked up his kist, stowed it under one arm, and walked off through the steer of folk, now gathering into tight knots around the steadings, or nipping away for their cars and a quick drive to the Auld Mill. Bill was heading for his wife's refreshment table, where a couple dozen folk were milling about, drinking and eating her cheese sandwiches. I got my jacket down from the nail I'd hung it on in the tractor-shed, then followed after Bill, who was reaching for something inside his jacket.

. . .seemed to be going high enough, Sandra was saying, pouring a cup of tea out for Bill.

He snatched it up, slunged the contents out on the grass in a brown steaming arc, and filled it back up with whisky. He raised the hip-flask to his mouth, screwed it round till the top held in his teeth was tight-fastened on, then slipped the flask back inside his jacket.

That was a long spell of heavy lots, I said, coming up beside him, nodding at Sandra. That bag of cement! Thirsty work.

Bill took a slurp of whisky. Have a cup of scaud then, he said, and slurped again.

I took a look at him. His eyes were fixed on the drink, and there was no possibility of him offering me a slug. Probably he wasn't really seeing me or Sandra yet, cause we weren't holding up a finger or nodding to bid, but at least his eyes were fixing on something now, not jumping around all over, and he was standing still, not jogging on the spot. Slowly he was beginning to gather himself, to come back to earth – as if it took half an hour after stepping down from the rouping kist for his feet to hit the ground.

Sandra slid a cup of tea across the table towards me. Aye, the prices sounded good, she said.

Good for who? said somebody behind me, and laughed. Good for the Murray Marts' percentage! It was the mannie Ronaldson, Roosty's father. He came forward between me and Bill and chapped on the table with his knuckles. Service! he cried, but I saw him wink at Sandra. She wasn't hurrying anyway.

Bill slowly turned and looked at him, blinked, then said, Here man Howbrae, here's service till you. He fished out his hip-flask and passed it over to Ronaldson, who screwed the top off and raised it to his lips. He paused.

By God, Murray, he said, You're surely getting genteel in your old age, taking your dram out of a plastic cup! What's wrong with a good old scoof out the bottle? He demonstrated.

Bill shifted a bit, shrugged his shoulders. Some right funny folk turn up at sales these days, with funny ideas on what a roup's all about. You never ken who's going to be watching you, and what they're going to be thinking

Have to keep up the public image, eh? I said. Maintain consumer confidence.

What? said Bill. As long as my bunnet's on straight, that's all the public image I need.

Saves splashing out on a comb, I suppose, said Sandra. Straight whisky and a straight bunnet: what more could a lassie ask of her man?

Ronaldson was laughing and pointing at his own head. He's lucky he's got hair to worry about! he cried. There were a few sandy-coloured strands behind his ears and just above the crease of his neck, but apart from that only smooth stretched skin.

Bill looked at him for a second, stopped his spluttering, and laughed. I'm not worried about that, you buggers! I'll tell you what I am worried about though: where did Dod get that model of the Eiffel Tower, the one that lights up in the dark? Did you see it?

197, I said.

Oh aye, said Ronaldson, A big brass thing. Would've been pricey, new.

Aye, and what was it doing hanging up in the byre? I said. I reckon it must've been one of the nowt had been to Paris. More likely than Dod ever going there, from what I've heard.

Dod was a bide-at-home right enough, said Bill.

God aye, said Sandra. He only ventured to Aberdeen once a year, and that was just to get his rickety hip x-rayed.

Aye, but listen, said Ronaldson, leaning forward on the table, and looking round at the three of us. I ken for sure he's been as far as London.

Never! said Bill, and took the flask from Ronaldson's hand, filled his cup, and palmed it away inside his jacket.

I mind the time fine. . .

Oi, Mrs Murray, any more milk on the go? someone shouted from along the table.

Sandra sprang back towards the porch. Wait for me, Howbrae, she said, then ducked inside, soon reappearing with two bottles of milk in each hand.

I mind the time *fine*, Ronaldson started again. A good few year ago now, it was, that I saw Dod of Goodman's comes trauchling away up to Howbrae. What's up Dod? I says. And he says, I've sold some neeps – you ken he had that girny peenging voice – I've sold a cartload of neeps to a chiel in London, but he wants me to deliver them, and I don't ken where it is.

What do you know? said Sandra, zipping back up to our end of the table, It's another one of Howbrae's yarns! Have I missed much?

Wheesht! said Bill.

So... said Ronaldson, holding up both hands for silence and looking us all in the eye. London? I say. You better head south, Dod. So he climbs back into his Fordson and heads off down the road, bogey behind him skailing neeps every bump he goes over. Well, after a while, he comes to a town. Is this London? he calls out to a woman in the street. Michty no, man, she replies, This is Fettercairn, you've a way to go yet. So Dod nods and waves and heads off south again, and after a long while he comes to a great big city. Aye aye, he thinks, and he asks a boy standing on a street corner, Is this London? The boy looks at him like he's daft. Hell no, he says, This is Edinburgh, fair on south! So Dod frowns and drives on. Govie dick, he thinks, It's a hell of a long road away from Blackden, this London place...

And he was right, I put in.

Shoosh, said Bill, I want to find out what happens.

So eventually, the mannie Ronaldson continued, Dod comes to this enormous big town, he can't see the end of it even. And sure enough, there's a sign at the side of the road: CITY OF LONDON.

At last! he thinks, and pulls over. There's a chiel walking down the pavement, bowler hat and briefcase, and Goodman's shouts at him, This is London, is it not? The loon looks back. Of course it is, he says. Well then, says Dod, Where do you want your neeps?

I burst out laughing, and so did Sandra. Ronaldson looked from one to the other of us, grinning, chuckling, Ha! Eh? Ha!

Aye aye, said Bill, rubbing his chin, Interesting... Do you think there'd be a good price for North-East neeps down there?

Me and Sandra and Ronaldson laughed more, till Bill turned away, tossing his empty plastic cup to the ground and raising his two hands to swat away the laughter from his ears. I'm away to the bog, he cried, and stomped off.

Watch your language, man, Ronaldson shouted after him. Lava*tory*, surely? Mind the public image!

Bugger that! Bill shouted back. You've been speaking pish for the last ten minutes, I'm surely allowed to go and have one! He disappeared round the corner of the house.

I'd got so wrapped up in the story that I'd forgotten my reason for coming over to the table in the first place. Here, Sandra, could I get a couple sandwiches, please? I said, before Ronaldson could get started into another yarn.

What's up, Paddy? she replied. Where's your own theday? You always have your own dinner.

Ach, my mother usually makes my piece up for me, see, and she's away for the weekend.

Dear oh dear, said Sandra, walking along to the other end of the table and picking up a paper plate with a few sandwiches still lying on it, grated cheese starting to spill out from them in wee curls. What about that then, Ronnie? she said as she came back and dumped the plate in front of me. The poor loon's just lost without his mammy!

It's not that, I said. I could easily've. . .

It's a shame really, said Sandra. Good job I'm here, eh Paddy?

It's just that I forgot last thing yesterday, and by the time I'd. . .

Here, said Sandra, Have three, have as many as you like, have them on me.

He'd surely be better having them on a plate, said Ronaldson, and the pair of them started sniggling.

I picked up two sandwiches and dropped fifty p on the money pile.

Christ, is this National No Sense of Humour Day or something? said the mannie Ronaldson.

Ach, I'm just. . .needing my dinner, I said. And a bit of peace and quiet to eat it in, after all the din, ken. I picked up my tea and walked away.

Exsqueeze me for breathing! Ronaldson said behind me. What a life without a wife, eh!

And what would you ken about that, Ronnie, Sandra was replying as I went out of earshot, You who's been happily married for thirty year. . .

I walked fast, didn't turn into the court, kept on along the track in front of the steadings, breenging on till I came to the end, where it opened into the stubble park with Dod's tractor and other implements spread out in neat lines. Half a dozen farmer folk were wandering about there, examining engines, shoogling bits of loose panel, shaking their heads. I paused, took a deep breath, and held it. Faintly, faintly, I could hear the sound of running water. I looked off to my left; the Black Burn was half a mile away, and buried at the bottom of the den; surely I couldn't be hearing that? I looked to the right: no sign of water, but out the back of the byre, set on the slope a few metres back from the track, was a small stone bothy.

The wooden door of the bothy was swollen with damp, and I had to lay down my tea and sandwiches to shoulder it open. But inside the air smelt dry and dusty, and me barging in set currents swirling across the room, raising clouds of dust to float and circle in the sunlight angling through the window. I took in my food and shut the door behind me.

My granda lived in a bothy like this when he was young. After leaving school, thirteen years old, he was taken on as orra loon at seven pound for a six-month fee at a big farmtoun at Strachan. He mucked out the stirkies' byre, washed the guano sacks on the rocks by the Feugh, and made the horsemens' brose in the morning. (And his cooking's never progressed beyond that – pouring boiling water over fine oatmeal, stirring once and serving – which is why I suppose my mother has to take grub intill him now.) The second six-month fee he got called a halflin instead of a loon, but the jobs were the same orra ones as before. At the end of that job, the farmer offered him the job of third horseman – thirteen pound for a six-month – but my granda wasn't happy. Maybe he'd seen enough of the horseman's life by this time, out in the cold and wet at every dawning, the horses worth more to the farmer and better cared for than the men ever were. Anyway, he told the farmer that he wasn't happy with that pay for this life. You'll take the thirteen pound or I'll keep it myself! said the farmer. Okay-dokay, you keep it, said my granda, I'm leaving this sotter! And he walked out of the farming and never went back, walked to Aberdeen and got a job with the council parks department. And it wasn't till the war came and he got sent to work in the Forestry with all the other gardeners that he came west again. And then he got married and his wife had a son, and then the war ended and they stayed on in Deeside and took over some old mannie's market garden business. Then, twenty-odd years later, my granda's son is delivering a load of tatties to the grocer's in Kincardine O'Corse when he falls in love with the lassie behind the counter, and three years later they marry, two more on and they have a baby daughter, a final two and they have a son as well. Then nothing for eighteen and a bit years, and then that son of the son of the ex-bothy-loon ex-market-gardener stands in a run-down bothy on a run-down croft on the edge of the Black Den, and wonders how he got there.

And maybe the answer is that sixty years before his granda had been a bit more clear-sighted or a bit more bold than most of the folk around him. He saw that horses were on their way out for good – even before the war he saw this – and that the horsemen were having a hell of a job switching to tractors, making a right hash of it, most of them. So he walked right out of the bothy, out of the farm, out of the life he'd been given, and he walked right on into a new life, a life of his own making.

I'd finished my first sandwich without tasting it at all. I took the second one out of my pocket and chewed on it slowly, working up cheekfuls of spit every few chomps to balance the dryness of the bread. As I ate, I looked around the bothy.

Goodman's had been worked by Dod himself for so long that it was hard to imagine that before mechanisation there'd been maybe two or three men as well as the farmer and his wife needed. There were two iron bedsteads against the walls still, though you can't be too sure of figures from that: more often than not more than one body would have to share each bed. The black iron fireplace was big enough for four or five folk to sit around. In the grate was a mixture of twigs and straw lying on a clump of soot, with more soot sprinkled on top: some bird's nest slipped down the lum. Imagine sitting in your house minding your own business, when suddenly the whole thing collapses under you and you're left sitting on nothing, your home disappeared down a big black hole! Could be worse, I suppose, if the fire was lit, and you fell down into the blaze along with your house.

Under the bothy window was a thick-legged wooden table, the top of it covered in dust, spattered with bird-shit; my plastic cup of tea was sending up a curl of steam from the middle of it. I went over, lifted the cup, and drank, gazing out through the cracked and cobwebby window. The bothy, at the end of the croft steadings, looked a little south of east, straight across to the den and the hills beyond it. Now, just after midday, the sun came slanting in from the right-hand edge of the window, falling in a straight line across the tabletop, and warming my skin as I held out my hand. I drew my finger through the dust on the table, marking a straight line along the edge of the sunlight.

On one side the worn and bleached wood was warm to the touch and bright in the sun, the pirls and flowings of the grain clear to see, lumps of dirt and odd nails, straws, smears of white bird-muck casting small shadows across the light-brown surface. But just a finger's breadth away, where the sunlight wasn't falling, across that sharp line, the tabletop was in deep shadow, the wood a murky greyish-brown, and there was nothing to be made out. The shadows hid the grain of the wood and the scatters of dirt layered over it.

For the first time all day, I started thinking about the ongoings of the previous night. The road to work had been so clear and sharp and sunny that memories of the dance and afterwards had never entered my mind, and once the roup had started there hadn't been a second free in my brain for them to slip in sideways,

111

even. But now, with my dinner eaten and nobody else around, and the thick quiet air of the bothy making my thoughts sound loud in my skull, now I kept seeing pictures of the night before:

Me walking into the Mill to find Dek and Bri buggered off; arriving at the dance to get slagged left, right and centre; struggling back with the stovies to find they'd fucked off once more. . .

And after that there was a second lot of pictures: Shona sweating as she hammered the mallet down on the steaks; Shona swiping hair away from her face as she sat in the door of her car; Shona going all dwammy as she drove, as she told the story of strange naked dancing in the woods. . . Her kissing me on the cheek, her saying she was as good as finished with Bobby Bastard, her saying she'd see me at the party this evening, her smiling and saying goodnight. . .

Blood was flowing into my cock, I could feel it growing, and Shona was smiling and saying goodnight. My cock was hardening and starting to heat, and a bunch of crazy women were dancing around in no clothes. My cock was pressing hard against the inside of my jeans, Shona was dancing naked in front of me, my hand was reaching down to unzip my spaver and bring out my hard-on as Shona was. . .

Shite, man!

. . .somebody was shouting outside the bothy, and my face took a beamer, and more folk were laughing in reply to the first shout outside, and I was evening out my breath, picking up my plastic cup and taking a sip of the cold stuff inside, and casually glancing out the window. A group of farmers was standing on the track just below the bothy, talking and laughing, and every so often pointing back to the park of implements where half of them had just come from inspecting the laughable machinery.

My cock was still hard, my face was still beaming. I had the idea that if I stayed looking out the window one of the farmers would sooner or later turn and see me and say, Hey, there's the auctioneer's apprentice HAVING A WANK! and my life would be over. I turned away from the window and crossed the floor to one of the iron bedsteads. There was no mattress, but I sat down on it anyway, the skeleton and springs of the thing jabbing into my backside, and tried to think of something else completely than Shona and witches and naked dancing in the. . .

When my granda lived in the bothy, he slept on a caff-bed which he made himself. The men would wait till the thrashing machine came round at the end of the harvest, puffing steam and smoke, and at the end of the day's work with it they'd collect armfuls of the caff that had been thrashed off the corn and they'd stuff it into their bed-ticks. That's what was called a caff-bed. And to start with, my granda says, you'd have a big lump in the middle of the mattress, but over the months that would flatten out as the caff rubbed down and settled. Then the problem would be when the caff-beds got too many months old, they'd give off a hell of a stew when you lay down on them, and you'd be near choking as you tried to get some rest, with no chance of a fresh refill till the end of the next harvest. Still, my granda says, they were hell of a lot more comfy than horsehair mattresses: awfully hard those buggers.

And awfully hard my cock had been, though now it was settled back at rest, thank God. But still my mind was filled with pictures of Shona when there wasn't anything else being forced through it. And one or two pictures of Dek and Bri too – they were not so welcome.

I got up from the bedstead, the springs creaking and twanging, and crossed to the table by the window. I was still holding my plastic cup, with a couple cm. of cold tea in the bottom, milk-fat puckering across its surface; I crumpled the cup in my fist and tossed it over my shoulder. I didn't see where it landed. I wasn't bothered. I was examining the tabletop again with its brightness and shadow, its woodgrain and dirt.

Things come to an end, things change. Folk that you've known for years – known them in games and at school, in fights and in laughs, drunk in the pub or on their best behaviour at the Sunday School, folk who've stayed at your house and you've stayed at theirs, you've camped out in tents with and in gang huts and in dens you built together – these people change, and so do you. Even Dek's mother had seen it. You see them clearly, these folk, every wee detail. Every good point and bad point, you see them all brightly lit if you look, you can make out everything about them.

But just cause you can make out everything, doesn't mean you want to keep on looking at them all the time. Cause there's other folk too – folk you don't really know, have glimpsed or talked to once, a friend of a friend, or a total stranger – and you're in the dark about them, only know the vaguest things about what they're like or how they think and feel, but these are the folk that start to interest you. You're fed up of the sunlight on the faces you've memorised, you want to cross over and be in the darkness, be with the folk who are new and unknown.

The sun had shifted. The line I'd drawn in the dust had been left behind. The shadow was advancing across the tabletop. Darkness was coming to get me and I was glad.

From the park full of cars, and the implement park, folk were converging on the court. I walked with them.

Roosty Ronaldson had turned up, and was standing in the sun outside the cart-shed door with his father. Both of them were smoking, both with a fag pinced between the thumb and forefinger of the left hand and then covered over by the curl of the other fingers. Both stood with all their weight on one leg, the right, both tapped the ground every few seconds with their left foot. But the mannie Ronaldson was bald as a beetle, and Roosty was hairy as a highland cow.

They were talking as I passed, so I just nodded and carried on, but Roosty cried after me, Hey man, Paddy!

Aye? I turned back to them.

That bugger of a boulder. . .

The one we couldn't budge?

Ronaldson snorted a laugh, looked me up and down.

Aye, went on Roosty. I got the digger to the brute, ken what I found?

I shrugged.

Not much wonder old Goodman's didn't shift it: the bastard's big as a house! Just about couped the JCB trying to get in under the thing for a bittie leverage!

That's a pain, right in the middle of your park. You should get a rebate on your rent for it.

The mannie Ronaldson snorted again. Dod Goodman was a sleekit old bugger right enough! Haw, I bet he kent that stone was there all the time, all the time he was going on about what a bargain price he was letting the ground to me at.

Roosty nodded. Aye, he wasn't daft, Dod.

He might've been a guffy old cunt, but he wasn't daft.

I laughed. Bit of a hummer, was he?

Well, have you seen a bath about the place? No chance, loon! I mind saying to Dod one time – I passed him in the car, him

115

singling neeps down by the road there, so I stopped for a news – I said to him, Christ Dod, you could surely do with a wash, man, you're fair guffing! And this was from ten feet away. A wash? he says. Do you think it? Michty aye, I say. Well, it's queer you should mention it, says Dod, For I broke the ice on the horse trough this very forenoon to do just that. But it was that cold I never got beyond taking my boots off. Govie dick, I thought to myself, There's nobody here to smell me but the beasts, and I don't hear them complaining!

Roosty laughed. You're making it up now, dad.

What! Ronaldson looked outraged. I swear to God, hand on my hernia, it's the truth.

Ha!

No, it just goes to show you, said Ronaldson, What happens when there's not a woman around to look after you. Dod never married, and his mother was long gone... He started sniffing, twitching his face around. Here, he cried, and ended up sniffing straight at me. Let's hope the wee Hunter's mammy isn't away much longer, or he'll end up just as sad and minging!

Ronaldson snorted with laughter, and Roosty grinned along with him.

Ach, get to...

Patrick! It was Sandra Murray. She'd been dotting about behind the trestle-table pouring out tea and selling the last few sandwiches, but now she was waving me over.

I better get on, I said.

See you later, said Roosty, still grinning.

Aye, and if you find any bars of soap on your travels about the place, you make a good offer laddie: they're guaranteed to be good as new!

*

Sandra had only been calling me over to say the afternoon session was about to begin and I'd better hash on. I'd've been there five minutes quicker if she hadn't hauled me over to tell me to be quick, but it wouldn't've done me any good to explain that to her. Something I learned early on with the Murrays was that it's one of the orra loon's jobs to make the bosses look smart and on the ball. So even if they're acting thicker than shit on a stick it's best just to nod and grin and get on with it. So I did.

It only took half an hour to get through all the lots in the house: Dod had restricted his junk-hoarding to farming gear. The house wasn't big, and the kitchen and two rooms were far from full, once all the rubbish had been cleared out. I'd spent half the morning before the start of the auction binning the stacks of damp-rotted copies of the *Press and Journal*, none of them more recent than 1979, that were piled up all round the walls. I'd also had to chuck a couple bags of foosty clothes and blankets from the bedroom, and more from on and under the ancient settee that filled half the front room, its grallochs hanging to the floor. It looked like Dod had been sleeping there a good while: fit to run a croft, but not to climb the stairs to his bed at night.

The circle of bidders was gathered round the back door, Bill Murray up on his kist in the middle of them in full flow. Revived by his dinnertime sandwiches, or maybe by the sups from his hip-flask, he was whipping the bidding along at a fair old speed, and I had to be constantly running to keep up with him. Cardboard boxes of old crockery, assorted battered pans, a girdle, a stack of old framed photos of men in suits and uniforms and women with the look of Queen Victoria, a big leather-bound bible, six boxes of unused candles. . . I carted them all out from their chalk-numbered places on the table and stone floor of the scullery, and held them high as I walked round the ring at Bill's feet.

But my mind wasn't entirely on the job now – bits of it kept slipping away to the bothy or the woods or Dek at the dance or Shona in her car – and I just about dropped a big old radio to the cobbles when its cloth flex fell and twisted round my ankles. My shoulder banged on the doorframe as I tottered over, then Bill reached over and grabbed me upright with a handful of shirt-collar, still grinning for the benefit of the crowd but swearing at me under his breath.

Sorry, I said to him.

You're doing fine, he said, But don't slow up. It's better fun the faster you go. . .

He launched into selling the radio, his lips a blur with the speed of the bidding, and I stood with the thing clutched to my chest, turning this way and that, my breath misting on the top of its dark wooden casing then fading away, misting over then fading away, misting and fading. And then the radio was sold for twentythree pound: buying fever breaking out again.

As I passed back into the scullery with the radio, I heard Bill announcing that the next lot I'd be bearing out would be an electric cooker in full working order. I just about dropped the radio again on the spot, till I looked around and spotted the appliance in question: one of those tabletop jobs with two wee rings and an oven the size of a shoebox, designed for folk who live off fried eggs and reheated mince pies. I carted it out the back door, held clear above my head.

Shortly after that, all the mobile lots from inside the house were sold or consigned to the junk-heap, and Murray stepped down off his kist, instructing any interested parties to proceed to the interior, where he'd be auctioning off an antique – and extremely comfortable – horsehair settee, a clock that was either a grandmother, or, by the looks of it, a great-great-grandmother, and a king-sized wrought iron bedstead with, which he believed had been smiddied by the same man who put up the 1897 Jubilee Fountain in Blackden square. Half the folk who went into the house were laughing, and half looked like kids being invited into Santa's grotto, but Bill grinned at them all and waved them on in.

Here, Paddy, he said to me, as the last few went past us. Hold onto this for a minute, will you, son? He thrust his kist against my chest, half knocking the wind out of me. I won't be needing that inside, he went on. And I won't be needing you either: there'll be enough of a stramash in here without you hytering about as well. So the two of you, just wait here a minutie, eh?

I went to say okay, but he'd already strode into the house at top speed, and his voice rose up above the babble of the others as he won into the front room.

I didn't listen, but just stood there feeling a bit daft, and looking around the court. The pile of unsold junk had grown high in one corner, and the mannie Brindle was poking about in it with a stick. He'd been hanging about all day, not actually bidding for anything, just standing at the back of the crowd smiling at people and going, Marvellous! Excellent! to himself from time to time. There were other folk hanging about too, a few of them taking the chance to stick their noses into the various out-buildings, some starting to head along to the implement-park beyond the bothy, a few trying to cadge a last cup of tea off Sandra. But Sandra was shaking her head, laughing at them, and shoving the crumpled plastic cups and wrung-out teabags and sandwich-wrappings into a binbag. She tied the top, and came walking over towards the back door of the house. She stopped when she saw me standing there, the kist in my arms.

What's this? she said. Free box to all who enter?

No, I said. It's Bill's kist.

I can see that, but why are you standing here with it?

I was going to stand *on* it, but my boots are a bit dubby.

She frowned. It's one thing Bill being in a good mood and letting you bosie the thing, but it's something else you standing on it. Don't push it, Paddy. It'll be a year or two down the road afore he'll be letting you up on his kist!

Well, at least I've got something to look forward to.

All I'm saying is, it's a responsible position up there.

God aye: you could fall off and break your neck!

Sandra sighed, shook her head, and ducked into the scullery.

A second later she reappeared without the bag of rubbish. Are you feeling alright, Paddy? she said. You don't seem yourself, somehow.

I shrugged, bringing the top of the kist up to knock against my chin. I don't ken who else I'd be except myself, I said. I'm the loon that stands around with a sharny box in his hands, that's who I am. The orra loon, that's me, eh? What else am I? Nothing. Not in the hours of work, anyroad. And outside them, who knows? Who cares!

There was silence for a second, then, So you're just waiting for Bill to come back?

Before I could answer, there was a loud noise of boots through the house, and voices coming our way, and Bill came out the door at the head of a stream of bidders. He slowed slightly to snatch the kist from my arms, then marched on again across the court. Thankyou sir, he shouted over his shoulder. Now have a break to recover! I'll manage the machinery fine myself... And he disappeared along the track towards the bothy park, the bidders trailing along behind him like kids after the Pied Piper. At the end of the line wasn't a laddie on crutches, but the mannie Ronaldson.

He winked at me and Sandra as he passed. He's on good form

theday, he said, nodding after Bill. More laughs than an afternoon at Pittodrie!

Cheaper as well, seeing as you never buy anything, said Sandra, but Ronaldson was already out of hearing. Terrible man that, she added to me. All mouth and no trousers.

I turned away. Well, you'd know, I said.

What?

Nothing, I didn't speak.

Aye. Well. Come away round and help me get this urn emptied and the tables folded and into the van.

Right-o, I said. I'll just nip and empty *my* urn first. If that's okay with you like, boss. Is it okay? Boss?

No answer. She was away. I went in to the lavvy.

When I came back out, the court was empty, except for the mannie Brindle, who was leaning against the wall next to the pile of unsold junk. I started round the side of the house, but before I got more than three paces there was a loud cough from him. I looked over. He'd lifted his arm and was beckoning me with his fingertips like I was a fucking waiter or something. Sandra was out of sight in the porch, and there was nobody else about: he was definitely meaning me. I dropped a tongueful of spit on the ground, pleitered my boots up and down in the dubs around it a couple times, then turned and walked over towards him, staring down at the patterns of mud across my toecaps.

I raised my head. Mr Brindle, I said.

He looked at me, nodded. Patrick, isn't it? he said.

Aye, Patrick Hunter. I work for Murray Marts.

I know who you work for, Patrick. I've been watching you.

You what?

Are you going to move on to be an auctioneer yourself then, in due course?

Eh, well, that was the idea. Whenever the Murrays give me a start at it, like. Hih, could be years yet! I looked round the court to make sure Sandra wasn't listening; she was still doing something to the urn, making the windows of the porch steam up.

Brindle was nodding again. I was listening to you talking just there. I would say you'd make an excellent auctioneer.

What, cause I can blab on a bit you mean? It takes a bittie more than that!

I'm sure, but. . .

But that is what they said at school, right enough: You're a hell of a blether, Hunter, and sharp enough to cut yourself – you might as well get paid for doing it.

So you were apprenticed to the Murrays?

It was either that or go into politics.

He looked serious. Politics. I see.

That was a joke, I said.

Ah! Good! Hmm. He looked over my shoulder at something or nothing. I started to think about how folk were always doing that to me these days, as if there was always something really interesting going on that I was always just. . .but he broke in again. Yes, Patrick, you've definitely got a way with words.

Hih, I've got away with a lot of things! I laughed, and Brindle did too, till there was a shout from the other side of the court.

Oi, Paddy! Don't bother Mr Brindle! Come and help me get this table folded.

I felt my face starting to go a bit red, and I shrugged at him and started to turn away. But he tilted his head on one side, put on a big smile, and said, very loudly somehow, but without shouting,

Mrs Murray, I wonder, could you spare me Patrick for a moment? He's being extremely helpful.

Sandra was paused at the back door with the urn in her hands. Well, if you're sure he's not being a pest. . .

Not at all, Mrs Murray, not in the slightest.

I'm not, I said.

Well five minutes then, she said, And then I'm needing you round the front, laddie.

I'll make sure he gets there, Mrs Murray, said Brindle, and gave her a big smile. She disappeared inside the house. Now, where were we? he went on. Ah yes, come with me a moment, Patrick. He put his hand on my shoulder.

What is it? I said, taking a step back.

It's business, he said. There's something I want to show you.

Eh, listen, if it's anything business you'd better talk to Sandra there, or wait till Bill gets back from the implements even. I'm just the orra loon.

He smiled. No, you misunderstand. Come with me and I'll show you something that could be to your advantage.

I looked at him. Has somebody left me something in their will? Old Dod? I only met him once! He stuck his hands in the pockets of his waxed jacket, then walked away from the pile of junk and towards the far corner of the house. After a second I followed him.

Brindle had stopped by his big Volvo estate, and was lifting the rear door as I caught up with him. The back seats had been folded down, and the whole inside of the thing was full of cardboard boxes, some folded shut, some open, with cardboard tubes and coloured files lying here and there on top.

What do you think of that then? he said as I came up.

I leant over and looked in the nearest box. Postcards, I said.

Ah-ha! Postcards! And there's more: tea-towels, calendars, desk-diaries. . . And they've all got my photos on them.

I looked at him. What, there's pictures of you on all this stuff?

Ha! No, pictures *by* me, photos I've taken of Scotland's beauty spots – and some of her black spots too!

You're a photographer?

He hooked a thumb into a buttonhole on his jacket. I was a photographer, he said, But no more. There's no money in that racket, not enough, anyway. So from scratch three years ago, I've diversified and built myself up into the fourteenth-largest producer of picture postcards and associated goods in Scotland!

I pursed my lips, and sucked in a loud stream of air. He seemed pleased at my reaction.

One starts off with the standards, of course: Balmoral Castle, Bonnie Banks of Loch Lomond, Shaggy Cattle Looking Over a Gate, but with a bit of luck and a lot of acumen one can branch out into more artistic areas before long.

He looked at me, a cheesy smirk on his face. I nodded.

Look at this, he went on, This series has been my pride and joy over the last season: giant luxury towels of Great Scottish Battlefields of the Olden Days.

He dug into a box of stuff over the left wheelarch and pulled out a big tufty towel with a colour photo of a stretch of grass and heather printed on it. It glowed green and purple.

Culloden! he cried, waving the thing in front of me like a bullfighter.

Very nice, I said.

He yanked out another one. Bannockburn!

1314, I said.

Exactly, he said, bundling the two battlefields together and bunging them back into the car. These things go like hotcakes to the tourists trying to find where their Scottish ancestors died and so on.

I laughed. Silly buggers, eh!

Not at all, not all, he said, frowning. Have respect for your customers, that's the first lesson in the business school of life. What's more, this line has also been very popular with us Scots.

Us Scots?

Certainly. Imagine you're abroad on holiday – Spain, Florida, wherever – and you're down on the beach pulling out your towel for lounging and lying on. And what's on the towel? A marvellous full-colour depiction of one of the picturesque sites of our glorious military history. Imagine your swelling pride as the Germans and the Scandinavians look on enviously with their Snoopy designs and their Stars 'n' Stripes rolled under their arms!

Listen. . . I checked my watch. I reckon I better be getting along, Mr Brindle. Sandra did want me to help her with the table and that, so. . . He looked disappointed. I mean thanks for showing me your pictures. I'm impressed. I've never seen anything like them.

He smiled, put his hand on my shoulder again. Good, he said. Now wait one second.

Well, what is it? I mean I really should. . .

He glanced around the court, as if checking for spies. There was nobody about. From the bothy park the faint sound of Bill Murray shouting bids at the top of his voice came drifting round the steadings. Tapping a finger to his nose, Brindle leant deep inside the Volvo and rummled around amongst the boxes there. Then he stopped, and mumbled something at me over his shoulder.

What? I said.

He spoke again, but still in no more than a whisper. Come in here and see this.

I sighed to myself, then stuck my head into the back of the car till it was level with his. He was breathing heavily with excitement, and the windows were starting to mist up. His hands were fidgeting on the flaps of a corrugated carton, his long nails making scratching noises on the cardboard. He eased open the flaps. The box was crammed full of postcards, four by four: sixteen orange sunsets went blazing down behind sixteen enormous factories and sixteen squat blue chimneys.

Great, I said, then, after a few seconds, What is it?

It's Ravenscraig. Steelworks. Near Glasgow.

Oh aye. They're closing that down, eh?

Exactly, Patrick, exactly. This is my lead series for next season: The Sun Sets on the Great Scottish Industries! What do you think?

Eh, I'm not sure. Is it not a bittie depressing?

Ah-ha, but look at this. He flipped one of the top cards over and stabbed at it with his finger. The motto says it all. Read!

I read it out. '. . .but the sun's aye risin' somewhair. . .'

It's good, Patrick, isn't it, you have to admit? It's poetry!

I stared at the card. Eh, aye. That really is. . .amazing, Mr Brindle. I mean in a way it's a memorial to the industries of the past, but then you read the motto and you think, Oh aye, just cause it's economic midnight here, well, the sun's probably coming up somewhere else. Korea, or Kent, likely. Three cheers!

I knew you'd get the point of it, Patrick, I knew right away. I said you were good with words, and here you are, by jingo, getting the drift of my poetic mottoes within seconds. Well done, lad!

He was talking far too loud now for being inside such a small glassed-in space, and his voice was booming in my lugs. Do you mind if we kind of reverse into fresh air for a minute, Mr Brindle?

I'm bowled over by that card, I really am. I need some more oxygen in my brain to cope with it.

He grabbed my arm. We can both leave this car as soon as you do one thing for me, Patrick. He turned his long chinny face towards me, looked at me through half-closed eyes.

I suddenly had the idea that he was going to ask me to kiss him. What's that? I said.

I think you know what I want, he said.

I don't, I said, I don't ken at all.

Patrick, I want you to say you'll come and work for me at Brindle's Bonnyview Cards.

What!

I need you, Patrick, you and your way with words, your knack of putting a sentence or two together. I need you to come and make up mottoes for the rest of my post-industrial postcards! I taxed my brains for this one, and I'm pleased with it, but it's not really my forte. I'm more of a snap-snapper and a wheeler-dealer, to be honest. I'm not really too handy with words. That's where you come in. There are going to be ten in the series. The problem was which images to select: there were so many sites to choose from! The ruins of Seafield Colliery, the bit of sea where the Piper Alpha platform used to be, the Linwood wastelands. . .dozens, dozens!

I slowly backed out of the car, stood up, stretched my back, and took in a few big mouthfuls of air.

And you'll pay me for this? I said, as Brindle came out of the car too.

Pay you? Of course! Well, the scheme will. One of these government youth schemes, you know: marvellous help for the small businessman.

And this is going to be a full-time job, writing mottoes for postcards?

Ah-ha! Good question, Patrick, very sharp! He put one arm round my shoulder and flung the other out towards the steadings. See that old byre there? he said. That's going to be the nerve-centre of my operations. I'm going to have a darkroom in the hayloft, a small office with a fax machine and all the requisites where the milking stalls are now, and – most importantly for you – a big store and mailing room in the cart-shed, where you can make up the boxes of orders from all over the country, make up these little bits of Scotland into nice padded parcels, and get them ready for sending off to expectant shopkeepers and hoteliers right across the Tartan Belt. And that includes Glasgow, these days!

I blinked a couple of times, as if thinking.

And the beauty of it is, Brindle went on, a grin wide across his chops, The whole renovation will be financed by grants from the local authorities and European agricultural-improvement funds. We're a regeneration area here, Patrick, it's marvellous!

Aye, it is that. But just to skip back a bittie, to the bit about this job. What you're looking for really is an office-boy: I mean the motto-writing's a wee part of it really.

He considered for a second. Well. . . Actually, to begin with, what I'm *really* looking for is somebody to clean out the byre, get all the centuries of cow-shit washed out, all of the previous owner's rusting rubbish cleared out of the loft and the other buildings. Have you seen the state of the place? My God, it's a nightmare! I'd be embarrassed to let my architect set foot in the place – or even the *builders*! – till I get some of that muck cleared out. He sighed through his nostrils. A particle of something fell out of one of them. A terrible, terrible mess, he said. No way to run an efficient farm-unit at all. He gazed around the court. Not much wonder it failed.

It didn't fail, really, I said. Dod died.

He didn't seem to hear me. He was staring at the wall of the boil-house, where the rusting bones of an iron cartwheel hung from a spike; below it and to one side was a massive granite cheese-press, half grown over by nettles and grass. His upper lip curled, then he spun round and clapped his hands together.

So! What do you say, Patrick? Are you interested in the job? The motto-writing and the office-boy and the muck-shifting job?

But who knows what it could lead on to! I mean, if you show the proper attitude, I may even let you take on some of the telesales work that my wife handles at the moment, calling up potential new customers.

Aye, well. . .

He looked at me, narrowing his eyes again, like he was studying the sun going down over a steelworks. Mind you, he said, You'll have to lose that accent if you're to make yourself understood from Lerwick to London.

Gosh. Yes.

Come on, Patrick, what do you say? I'm a businessman, can't hang around. Decisions have to be made like lightning in Brindle's Bonnyviews! What's your answer?

Paddy! It was Sandra shouting from the back door of the house.

I turned to Brindle and shrugged. I'll have to think about it, I said. I'll get back to you, okay.

He clapped his hand on my shoulder once more. Do that Patrick, and soon! His eyes were glistening. Do boy!

The park below the steadings was emptying of cars, and the last few successful bidders were handing their cloakroom tickets to

Sandra, sitting in the passenger seat of the van with the receipt book on her lap and the cash-box in the glove compartment in front of her. Behind her the trestle-tables and the urn and all the rest of the Mart's gear was safely stowed away. She'd take folk's money, give them a receipt, then they'd wander off to pick up their lots and cart them off to their cars. Their shouts and laughter as they dumped their purchases in back seats or boots, and the sound of slamming car-doors and engines revving, carried clear up to me through the cold still air.

I leant on the fence at the front of the house and looked down at the cars as they pulled away over the stiff cropstubble towards the gate in the bottom corner of the park. The whole scene was giving me ideas. What I had to do was get an old wreck of a car from somewhere, find an empty field of grass, then just go round and round till I'd mastered the whole thing of driving. There'd be no dykes to smash the car against, no wee kids jumping out to get run over, no tractors reversing in front of me unexpectedly. . . And there wouldn't be the difficulty of steering along a narrow twisty lane; I could just swerve all over the place and it wouldn't matter. Then, after a few weeks solid practice in the park, I could get somebody to take me out on the roads – maybe a few lessons from the guy in Mortlich who calls himself a driving school, even – just to get the technical details in my head and a few rough corners knocked off before I went to sit the actual test.

Of course most folk I knew could drive already. Most folk even had their own motors, all the ones with jobs, anyway: that's the first thing they spent their wages on. Fuck's sake, Dek'd already got his licence and had it taken away again! Eighteen-months ban for drunk driving, stupid bastard, just six weeks after he'd passed his test!

The other *of course* was that a lot of folk hereabouts had been driving since they were about four: driving tractors about their dad's farm. I never did that. Pushing a barrowload of compost or carrots around the market garden was about all my dad ever let me do. That didn't do me much good now: an XR2 is much more impressive to the dames than rushing up to them saying, Do you want a hurl in my barrow? as they come out of the dance.

It was my old man's fault I never learned to drive, actually. I mean I don't hold it against him, he couldn't help himself. But the fact is, when I turned seventeen, instead of spending my evenings and weekends getting in driving practice like everybody else, I was having to visit my dad in hospital, or having to look after him when he was home, or look after my mum, even, cause my dad was wearing her down. Helen had learned to drive okay when she was the usual age, but six months later she went away to college down south. And what's the use of it there, where there's buses every five minutes and taxis for the asking?

The park below me was empty now, and there was no movement from the park next along to it either, a field of pasture. But after a few seconds I realised that it wasn't empty: half a dozen stirks were bunched in a far corner, standing stock still, their heads and necks stuck halfway between gawping up at the world around them and down at the grass in front of their noses. They looked kind of stunned. Maybe numb with the cold, or numb with the boredom of standing around month after month doing nothing but eating grass and trying to mount each other and getting fatter and fatter till finally they'd be carried away in a big transporter. At last! they'd be thinking, as they drove through the slaughterhouse gates, Finally something interesting is going to happen!

I really had to start saving something out of my wages every week, putting something aside till I could get some mobility, some independence.

There were noises behind me: the Murrays shouting at each other in and out the house. But no, it was only Bill yelling; now his voice was echoing around the court.

Paddy! Paddy! Where the fuck are you, loon?

I sprung up from my leaning-post and strolled into the court. Bill was standing just outside the back door, red in the face, flask in the hand.

I'm here, boss, been waiting for you: what's to do?

Come and get this fucking stuff shifted, he said.

What, the unsold junk? I was going to, but I didn't ken where till. I mean Sandra said to me earlier that Brindle didn't want anything left lying around, that he was going to start gutting the place and doing it up straight away.

Sandra said, Sandra said. . .

Was that not right like? I thought that was why we were telling everyone to collect their lots theday or they'd lose them. Sandra! I shouted towards the van at the far end of the court. Sandra, did Brindle not tell you that? That he was needing the place cleared? Sandra?

Bill sighed. She's not there, Paddy, she's away.

Away? I thought she was doing the cashing-up in the van?

He shook his head, raised his flask to his lips, and shook a last drop out of it, head tipped back. Nah, he said, She was, but she finished five minutes ago. Howbrae's giving her a lift home.

Ronaldson?

Bloody typical: once the folk've buggered off and the money's been made, who is it clears off with the cash? Her! And who is it's left clearing up the fucking leftover shite?

Eh, me?

He walked over to the pile of junk in the corner of the court and gave it a kick. The junk shifted with grates and clangs. Aye, me! he said. Sometimes I wonder: who's the auctioneer around here? Who's the fucking boss?

Not me.

Aye, not me. He looked down at the unsold stuff for a few seconds, then went to drink from his flask again, found it empty, and muttered, Traitor! while shoving it back inside his jacket. Then he looked up. But I *am* the fucking boss, so come on, let's get this hillock of shite away into the cart-shed and be done with it.

Right. I pulled my rigger-gloves out of my back pocket, got them on, and clapped my hands together. Is this the lot? Ten minutes humphing Bill, ten minutes! I went over and picked up the first thing I came to: an old lemonade box with a rough plug of rusty screws and nails in each compartment. Christ, I said, Somebody missed a bargain! Ten kilos of small brown metal things! All sorted into their different sizes as well!

Bill lifted a jutting tattie-sack. I'm too old for this, he said. I should be on the fucking golf course.

Bit dark is it not Bill? Have you got luminous balls or something?

What shite are you talking now? The contents of the sack settled and rattled as he crossed towards the cart-shed.

To help you see in the dark, like! On the golf course, ken?

Oh. Golf. I thought you were talking about getting your hole. What!

He laid down the sack. Nothing. Forget it. For a moment he concentrated on taking the bit of twisted wire out of the hasp; then he kicked the shed door wide, and propped it back open with the tattie-sack. Stick it right up the back, Paddy, otherwise we'll be out the door with shite afore we ken it.

That reminds me, I said, I better get my bike out afore we barricade it in.

I dumped the box of rust and went up to the back of the shed. There was a thick smell of diesel and old straw, but not much light. After a few seconds, my eyes got used to the dark.

Hold on, I said, Where's my bike?

There was no answer. Looking down, I could see a couple of its tyre-prints each side of a half-dried puddle of oil on the floor, but it wasn't leaning against the wall there. It wasn't leaning against any of the walls. I ran back outside; Bill was rooting about amongst the junk.

Hey, Bill!

He didn't look up.

Bill! I stood in front of him.

Don't stop now, lad, you've only just started.

Aye, but Bill, my bike's gone.

He straightened up with a crushed roll of chicken-wire in his arms. I'm not stopping to talk to you, Paddy. I'm needing home. He walked off.

Fuck's sake! I grabbed a couple of filthy-black five-gallon cans and chased after him. Something went gloop inside them with each step.

I left my bike in there first thing. . .

I told you, I'm not stopping to talk.

Aye, but I'm not stopping either. Talk to me while we're working, this is important!

I don't ken anything about it, he snapped.

I haven't said anything yet!

Aye have you: your bike. He stopped at the door of the shed and tossed the wire towards the dark end. And the only pusher I've seen all day was that knackered old message bike we sold this afternoon.

He turned back into the yard. I dropped the cans of black stuff just inside the shed and ran after him.

I never saw Dod on a bike, I said. Are you sure it was his? Bill went past me with some more wire: leaving the fine heavy loads for me. . . I crouched down, got my hands round a festering car battery, and staggered after him.

Of course it was Dod's, he said over his shoulder. I took it along to the park myself. I mean it must've been his, it was in his. . .aye. Well, it was in. . . I assumed it was his, cause it was in his cart-shed. He hurried past me.

I laid down the battery, and turned back again, flexing my fingers after the weight of the thing. He was coming towards the shed with another sack. I stepped in front of him. He stopped.

Are you telling me, Bill, I said, standing there, That you found a bike in the shed here? Not *two* bikes, one of which you moved to a safe place knowing it to be mine cause you'd seen me arrive on it every morning all summer? Are you telling me you found a message bike – the message bike I used to deliver fruit and veg for my dad on? The bike he used to deliver fruit and veg for *his* dad on? Are you telling me you found my bike, and wheeled it along to the bothy park, and sold it?

Eh. . . He shrugged. Aye, that's it, more or less.

Bill – fuck's sake Bill! – you auctioned off my bike! I rubbed my hands down over my face, black muck and battery acid no doubt smearing off my gloves.

He looked me in the eye for the first time. Sorry, Paddy, he said. I was a bittie out of sorts at dinnertime, what with Brindle driving through the middle of the roup and Howbrae acting the goat. Ken? He stepped past me, and into the shed with his sack.

Jesus Christ.

Still, look on the bright side, Paddy. I got a good price for it. He jinked past me and back towards the pile of shite.

I stayed where I was. How much?

135

He came past me with a couple of cracked and filthy demi-johns hooked in his thumbs. Twentyone, he said. Into the shed with them, back to the pile again.

I was stammygastered. Twentyone quid?

He passed me. Less commission, of course.

What!

Ten per cent of twentyone, two pounds ten, that taken away leaves. . .well, rounding it up seeing as it's you, eh: nineteen quid, straight into your pocket, no questions asked. Not bad really, for a machine of that age.

Not bad? But I didn't want it sold! What am I going to do with nineteen quid? I won't get another bike for that!

Bill shifted from one foot to the other in front of me. You could get a bottle of whisky, maybe. Two if you get a cheapish blend.

Three if I get meths!

He skittered off towards the pile of junk, half its original size now. I went after him, picked up a splintered pick-axe handle, didn't crown Bill with it. . .

Right, I said. It's a mistake, mistakes happen. We'll just find whoever it was bought it and explain to them and give them their money back and everybody'll be happy.

Well, if you're lucky. I mean, in the eyes of the law the bike belongs to them now.

Them? And who is them?

Eh. . .I can't mind off hand. You'd have to look it up in the receipt book, that should have the name and address.

And where is the magic fucking book then?

Och, Sandra's away with it. She's got all the paperwork and the cash and that. . .if Howbrae hasn't got his hands on her, I mean it yet, that is. He shook his head. I'm sorry, Paddy; I guess you'll have to wait till we're back in the office on Monday.

We stood by the scatter of junk in the corner of the empty court. The blue of the sky above was thickening into gloaming as I looked up at it. I took a series of deep breaths, drew the cold air into my hot lungs, wished I could screw the top off my skull and let the same cold air swirl about my overheating brain.

Jesus. I'm never going to see that bike again, it's gone forever. What a life. What a fucking life.

Bill reached out and clapped me on the shoulder. Tell you what, he said. I'll give you the nineteen quid now. Can't say fairer than that, eh? Out of my own pocket! I mean really you should get it from Sandra, but. . .fuck it, here you go loon.

I heard the crinkling of banknotes under my nose. Still I looked skywards.

And I'll tell you what else, I'll give you a lift home, Paddy, right to your door, how about that? Eh? The cash and a lift: how about that? Happy? Are you happy now?

Nah, stop the bus, Bill, it's alright.

He drove on. It's no bother, Paddy.

No, I ken, but I'm needing out. Stop!

He glanced over at me, slowing slightly. We're not halfway there yet loon. It's no hassle to drive you. It's on my way.

I'm needing out! Stop! I've just remembered something I forgot!

He checked his mirror and pulled into the side. Forgot back at Goodman's?

I had my belt off and was opening the door. Thanks for taking me this far, Bill, I said. I'll see you on Monday, probably. I got out of the van, stepped down, and went straight to the bottom of the ditch there. Shite!

Are you alright, loon?

Aye aye: it's dry, just full of leaves. I got to my feet.

No, but. . .

I've just minded, there's something I want to see, down in the den.

Bill started to speak again, but I slammed the door on him, raised my hand in a wave, and turned, started walking back the way we'd come. A second later he reversed past me, wheeched the arse of the van into a gateway twenty metres on, then steered out and away down the road. He gave his horn a couple of toots. Honk honk, I said back.

I crossed the road. Once the van was out of hearing, the rush of water from the bottom of the den could be heard quite clearly. I looked over the ancient fence, leaning on a paling-stab. Immediately below, the land fell sheer to a rocky bit of the burn. Odd bits of rubbish and fallen branches were strewn over the slope all the way down to where the dark water broke open in white sprays over jaggy outcrops and rough boulders. But most of the denside was covered in brown and yellow leaves and mats of red-brown bracken: slippier than a well-greased futret. The paling gave slightly, creaking. I leant off it and started walking back down the road.

Fifty metres on, the slope wasn't so steep, and the trees were close enough together that even if I did go sklite on my arse I'd be able to grab hold of one and stop myself sliding onto the rocks. I pulled on my rigger-gloves, pushed against the rusty top strand of wire, and straddled over the fence. The ground was slippery, but my big work boots had a good grippy tread on them. I started down towards the water.

When I was young I used to go down into the den all the time. Me and my sister, or me and my pals, we'd gather brambles down in the dark parts where they grew late but big and sweet. Something had gone wrong with the den these last few years, though. The ground was boggy and stinking now, and the nettles and bracken were wild in their growth, making the whole floor hellish to get through, your path blocked at every step, your skin stung and stabbed, your clothes snagged by the bony remains of the briers. So I never went near the den any more, hadn't done for ages. If there were still berries hidden down there, nobody picked them: they rotted where they grew.

I'd worked my way to the bottom, and across a narrow strip of boggy bank to the water's edge. I hunkered down there and got my breath back, looking around.

About a hundred metres upstream was The Dooker, where an outcrop of some hard white rock across the den caused the burn to back up and widen out, only continuing downstream after hanging around in a big dark pool, nearly as wide as the Mortlich swimming baths, deeper than the deep end there. In the old days, witches used to be put on trial here. The trial used to consist of having your legs and arms tied, then being chucked into the water. If you floated then you must've had supernatural powers: they hauled you out and burned you to death. But if you sank to the bottom and drowned, you were officially declared innocent: your body was dragged out and buried. Of course, nothing like that goes on these days.

The Dooker was also the place that all the Blackden kids used to come and swim in the summer. It was great on a hot day to come running down through the trees and dive right into the freezing water – less chlorine and bus-fares and attendants than the baths at Mortlich. Me and Dek and Bri used to tie bits of stick together, lumps of log, trying to build something that would float across a stretch of water we could swim in fifteen seconds. And the worst of it was, the things always sank! But it was a laugh, definitely a great laugh. The three of us wouldn't do that now.

Eventually the water poured out of The Dooker and on down the den. The fall where it curved over the white outcrop and down three or four metres to another smaller pool below was called The Black Slug, maybe because of the rounded shape the water made – like a slug's back – as it went over the rocks. But the water flowing along in front of me wasn't really black, it was various shades of brown, depending on how deep it was, and what was underneath. The brown was particles of peat, washed away and carried down from the sourcelands of the burn, high in the hills to the north of the village, above the Ronaldsons' Howbrae, high amongst the murky lochans and abandoned peatmosses there. Moulding over a bright granite slab at my feet, the water was clear, the colour of straight whisky. Further out, skirting a black-rotted stump of log washed down from some forestry works upstream and sucked to a halt in a patch of muddy sediment here, the water was darker, almost opaque, like quick-flowing treacle.

And away it flowed down the den, southwards through the broadening floor, spreading out into a series of curves and shallows, its edges softening into long areas of bog and dubs. There the ground was hobblie under your feet, hummocks of grass and cotton shuddering as you walked on them, mud all around wauchie and slerping, ready to suck the shoes off your feet if you slipped. It was treacherous ground for a mile or two, till the flat land ended and the long slope down to the big river began. The Black Burn got its act together before meeting the Dee: it had to look good for the tourists and the royals.

I wasn't going down there. But upstream didn't attract me either: in twenty minutes I'd be back at the village, right outside the Auld Mill to be exact.

I stood up, set my left foot firmly on the granite slab in front of me, the water still below lacehole level, then leapt with the right boot leading to purchase on the crumbling top of the log for a second, before lunging my whole body forward and falling onto my knees on the far bank. Something had moved underneath me, and now the water was slunging louder, moving faster. I got to my feet and looked. The log had been swivelled by my jump, and was lying with its narrow end to the force now, the water flowing quickly down and round it. And all the burn was drumlie and dark: my weight had dug the log down into the mud and churned it up into flowing black clouds.

I started climbing the slope in front of me, pulling myself up steep bits with grips on tree roots and handfuls of wiry bracken. Soon the trees were thickening around me, the ground was level, and I'd left the noise of the burn behind. I went on into the depths of the wood.

The light was beginning to fail, and I still hadn't found what I was looking for. The Kirk Wood isn't big, but it's very dense: that was the problem. It was slow work getting moved with my way constantly blocked by whippy, thorny branches tangled together at face level. I had to push a path forward with one arm held crooked out in front and the other hand shielding my eyes. Only so often when I came to a small clear patch where a tree had couped and died, or been choked by the height of the rotting layer of black dropped pine-needles round its base, could I pause and have a look around. And even then the denseness of the trunks and branches made it hard to see very far.

The wood was planted by the Laird of Corse during the First

World War, after he'd had to cut down just about all the standing trees on the estate. My granda told me about it. He was at school at the time, but all the pupils got days off to come and strip the bark off the trees that the foresters had felled. They got paid two pennies a tree. Then the timber was sawed up and shipped over to France to prop trench walls and line roads through the blood and glaur. By having his trees cut down, the laird was doing his bit for the war effort. And the following year he had new ones planted. Not just behind the kirk, but also between the school and the pleasure park, on the slopes all along the road from Blackden to Kincardine O'Corse, and in an enormous swathe from the edge of the village by the Shakkin Briggie right up to and beyond The Strath. In fact he had the new trees planted exactly where all the old felled ones had stood: the Big Beeting, it was called. My granda got more days off school; nine pennies a day, the planting.

But now the Kirk Woods were choking. There were fine big trees all around – mostly larch, with odd Scots pines and quite a lot of pale silver birks as well – but they'd never been managed, they were too close together, their branches locked and wrestling above. And all the second and third growth trees below were grey and spidery from lack of light. They straggled up towards chinks in the canopy, and died easily, bashed over in gales to tangle up with each other and the ferns and fungi sprouting from the rotted stumps of their forebears. The webs of jaggy branches and the tilting splintered trunks were like old barbed-wire and tank traps, or their ghosts, come back to haunt the place they grew up in.

Since 1919 the woods had been ignored; several lairds in a row had more interesting things to take up their time. It was only a couple years back that the present laird – *Young* Durward of Corse he's called, though he must be twice my age – took over the estate from his father, and started working his way through it with chainsaws and lorries with grabs and log-dragging donkeys for where the lorries couldn't reach. This time the sacrifice isn't inspired by love of king and country, but by love of tax rebates. Another difference is that the laird can't hire the local kids to work all day for peanuts. Then again, he doesn't need to hire kids nowadays: there's always a queue of folk volunteering for peanut duty whenever a job's on the go around here. But neither the young laird or his workers have got round to the Kirk Wood yet, so it's still lying thick and tangled and lifeless.

Up ahead was a patch of light amongst the dark trunks of the trees. I headed towards it. Bright green, the floor ahead was bright and green, which meant no more carpet of pine-needles and rotting leaves and ferns, but grass, green grass, grass open to the light of the sun. And there was the Sabbath Stane. I stopped. From a few metres inside the wood, the stone looked like it had grown there, a giant grey fungus. It was a couple of metres long, half as high, with a flat top. Moss and lichen crawled up the sides of it in green and brown patches.

I took a step forward. There was an explosion of sound in my face, twigs snapping and wings flapping and the cooshie-doo hooting out an alarm call of chokes and clucks as it threw itself away from me into the clearing then up into the empty air above the stone. I waited till I could no longer hear the bird, then cleared my throat loudly and stamped my feet a couple times to warn any other lurking creatures of my approach. Silence. Nothing stirred. If there was anything about, it wasn't moving – it was watching me.

I walked out of the woods and into the clearing. Right in the middle was the remains of a bonfire. I poked at it with the toe of my boot. A layer of dead leaves had been scattered over it, but a circle of black and grey ashes was clear to see, with fragments of charred and blackened wood sticking up here and there .

Something cracked out in the trees. I looked up, listened, waited. Nothing. When I started taking breaths again, I had to force myself to make them big, slow, long ones. I gazed around the clearing. It was empty except for the massive stone and this one firesite, but directly ahead of me, just under the trees, something else caught my eye. I stepped over. It was a big pine bough, as thick as my leg. One end of it was completely burnt away, and black marks of fire reached up the bark. Soot came away from the bunches of needles onto my hands as I held it up to the light.

I dropped it, and walked around the clearing, looking into the trees. There were two more big branches with charred ends. It looked like they'd been half-burned then dragged out of the bonfire, doused, and hidden in the dark of the woods. It must've been quite a blaze with all those on the go, but the thickness of the forest all around would've hidden the flames from the rest of the world.

I walked over to the stone and ran my hand over the top of it. There were hollows here and there, shallow circles the size of a nip-glass's base, eroded or carved out of the granite. I had a sudden memory-flash of coming across the Sabbath Stane one autumn morning, when me and Helen had skived off Sunday school together. She'd told me that this was the meeting-place of the witches for miles around, where they met to cast their spells and dance around and even KILL WEE BOYS ON THE SACRIFICIAL STONE! I was frightened by her stories, but made on not to be, and pointed out the hollows on top of the stone: Then these'll be for catching the loon's blood when you stab him through the heart, I said. Helen began to get feart, and within seconds the two of us were running for our lives, pushing through the trees, rushing back to the kirk to sit on its steps till the Sunday school ended and our dad came to collect us in the car.

I went back into the open of the clearing and sat down, my shoulders against the front of the Sabbath Stane, my feet touching the edges of the bonfire. The grass around me was springy and very short. It looked like it had been cropped by some animal, a sheep or a goat, though it was hard to imagine any beast less dumb than a human fighting through the woods to get here. I pictured the witch-women Shona saw struggling through the forest in the dark, no clothes on, branches scratching their skin, pine-needles pricking into their feet. Then I thought, no, they'd come here dressed as normal and strip of in the clearing, strip off naked and dance their dances, warmed by the flames of the bonfire, the sweet smell of roasting resin in their nostrils, the crackle of the blaze and their own chanting loud in the night as they danced and sang and. . .who knows what.

I picked up a bit of twig and started poking around in the ruins of the fire. There was nothing but ashes. What else could there've been? Bits of bones? Scraps of used durex? Somehow it seemed impossible to be a witch and also be into safe sex. They seemed to cancel each other out. But there was nothing anyway. I started drawing patterns in the fine grey wood-ash: circles, arrows, question marks. I wrote PATRICK, then changed some of the letters so it said WITCH – then I scribbled that out with the twig and drew the covering of leaves back over where I'd been writing. I looked around the wall of trees. The darkness was clotting beneath them, I couldn't see more than two or three deep into the woods now. The circle of sky above was still clear, but the blue was darkening. Soon I'd have to head back to the village, or risk wandering all night in the pitch-black forest.

I jumped to my feet, then cried out – my cock was standing and hard, trapped down the leg of my pants, the elastic cutting in. I loosened my belt and opened the spaver, and reached down to ease my ys out of their stranglehold. My cock swung up, released; I could feel the air cool on my hot skin. I moved my hand to rub the elastic burn. I rubbed it, my cock rose, I rubbed it some more, it rose more – there were several days worth of frustration inside bursting to get out – so I rubbed it again, looked round the clearing, pictured the witches dancing round the fire. Naked in the night I saw them dancing, round and round, singing and shaking, their breasts bouncing as they danced. And here came Shona, dancing with them, naked too, bouncing and dancing, light of fireflames licking her skin and licking and licking and bouncing and dancing and. . .I came.

My face was burning, but I was cold. My cock was already shrivelled. I gave it a shake and a drip flew off the end. I laid it back against my belly then pulled my ys up over it, then my breeks.

Fastening my belt, I gazed at the line of spunk I'd spurted out over the grass. It was already soaking into the soil, except for a few straggly blobs that were lying on the brown leaves over the bonfire ashes. It seemed funny to me, or maybe sad, that it could disappear so fast and with so little trace. In other circumstances that spoonful of spunk could've changed the world! Imagine if Hitler's old man had gone and had a quick wank instead of squirting it up his wife. . . Then it seemed sad and funny to me that I could even think of such a thing. I really was a sad and funny bastard at times, it had to be admitted.

In the old days, in Ancient Egypt or someplace like that, one way folk tried to tell the future – when reading the stars and watching flying birds and cutting open goats' bellies had failed – was getting their minister to whip out his thing and toss himself off. And the pattern of his spunk in the dust would be the shape of things to come. Cross my palm with silver!

I examined the pattern I'd left on the grass. It looked like nothing. Fuck that for a fortune telling.

I battled my way through the woods, ducking double now and then to bend below dense spreads of jaggy branches, rather than have my face whipped pushing through the middle of them. I was sweating and choking from kicked up leaf-mould, but before long I came to a narrow strip of land that hadn't been plantationed, though it had been naturally seeded by birk and broom and whins and was pretty clogged up. I turned left along it, and trudged on. This was the old drove road, the route travelled by herds of nowt in the old days, as they were being driven to sell at the great southern trysts. The drove road went right through the middle of the Kirk Woods, forded the Black Burn at the broad, boggy part of the den, then continued on to Mortlich and beyond. Probably it was used for every kind of traffic, not just droving, till the denside road was built a hundred-odd years ago.

As I walked along, I kept an eye out for footprints and broken branches, or other signs that folk had come along here in the recent past – like on the night of Halloween. But the ground was frosted hard and there was nothing to be made out. It was obvious that folk did come this way from time to time, though; an easy path could be threaded between the small trees and bushes, one that had obviously been trampled clear of vegetation over the years. But that could just be folk taking their dog for a walk, or kids skiving Sunday school.

Of course it's possible that this wasn't originally a drove road at all. Going back further than that even, maybe it was a military road, one of General Wade's jobs. Certainly there'd been some

Jacobite ongoings in these parts. Bonnie Prince Charlie's even meant to've stayed the night at Corse House with a few of his generals and chums on his way south to Edinburgh in 1745. That's what the Durwards of Corse like to put about, anyway. More than likely, though, it's just them trying to get their name in the history books, even if it's just for providing a high-class B&B.

The story goes, that after Charlie and his gang had marched off down the drive from Corse, through the big gates and away, the laird of the time was so overcome that he dang them shut with a crash and cried that the yetts of Corse would never again open till a Stuart king was on the throne of Scotland. And so it is that they've been firmly shut to this very day, the two sides so rusted together now that they probably couldn't be opened even if Rod Stewart was crowned king of the country. The Durwards make out that the laird of the day was a great Jacobite supporter, and giving some big heroic show of support for the cause. I'm not so sure, though. I reckon if he was anything like his descendant up at the house these days, what he was probably saying as he slammed the gates was, Thank God I'm rid of that poofy French bastard! Treating the place like a hotel! I'm not letting him back in till pigs fly and he's the king of the sty!

Whistling approached. A whistler must be attached. I stopped dreaming, looked around: the trees were dense on both sides, hard to win through. And probably too late anyway, for the sound of someone swishing through the bushes was only metres away and. . .as I stood there, the minister – black coat buttoned tight, white hair standing on end like he'd just seen the holy ghost – pushed through between two broom bushes.

Seeing me, he jumped, his whistle drying up into a sharp sook of breath. Eh. . .good day! He seemed about to back away into the undergrowth – his hands slipping out of his pockets and feeling behind him for a gap in the bushes or something – but for the moment he stayed stuck to the spot.

I straightened myself up, smiled, said, Hello, Mr Ritchie! in a cheery voice. Another fine night!

Eh, indeed, indeed. . . He peered at me through the gloom of the overhanging trees. I wasn't expecting to meet. . .eh. . . He laughed. The nights are certainly drawing in, aren't they?

Fairly that, minister.

He nodded and laughed again. I'm sorry, I don't quite. . . He put his head on one side and looked over my face; with his head tilted sideways, he could avoid the embarrassment of having to look anyone straight in the eye.

It's Patrick, I said. Patrick Hunter from The Strath.

Ah, Mr Hunter, of course. Yes indeed, very good. A pleasant evening for a stroll, is it not?

Hih, aye, aye. I was just in there having a look at the old Sabbath Stane. You ken the one I mean?

I certainly do, Mr Hunter, I know it well! A smile had come over his face, and his hands came round in front of his chest and rubbed their fingertips together. In fact I was examining it myself just a couple of weeks ago!

I looked at him, tried to imagine him without his coat and dog-collar, dancing round a bonfire. *Exactly* a fortnight ago, was it? I said, watching for his reaction. He frowned slightly, brought his forefingers up to his lips, then said:

Do you know, I really can't recall. But I do remember it was a rather wet and rainy morning. I was soaked when I got back to the manse! My wife gave me quite a telling off!

Ah, so it was in the daytime, was it?

Yes yes, and very interesting it was too. I'm writing a little pamphlet, you see, for the Blackden Community Council:

Historical and Natural Trails and Tales, it's called. His shoulders shook with the excitement of the project. And the Sabbath Stane really is a remarkable example of the continuity of worship on this spot over thousands of years. Originally, of course, there would have been an array of smaller stones standing in a circle in front of the one that remains now – the recumbent, as it is known.

I didn't ken that.

Yes indeed. No one knows the exact date, but it's only within the last two hundred years or so that the other upright stones were broken up and taken away. A great shame, really, to see any place of worship defiled in such a way. Though of course the faith of the sun-worshippers – if such they were – would have been very far away from anything we could understand or participate in. Ecumenism must have some limits, eh? Ha!

Whatever you say, Mr Ritchie. You're the expert.

But the coincidence really is remarkable, that only a few hundred yards away, five thousand years later, the good Christian people of Blackden 1873 should choose to erect their new kirk. Why did they choose this site? Was it to overwhelm the old pagan temple with the scale and grace of the new building? Or perhaps because of some instinctive feeling for this place as ancient holy ground?

Eh. . .

We shall perhaps never know, but speculation is. . .

Mr Ritchie!

He shut up, blinked at me a couple of times, then pressed his fingertips to his lips. Sorry, Mr eh. . .sorry. But it is a fascinating area!

Aye, I ken, it's just that it's been a long day, and. . .

Ha! There was an ambiguity there – did you notice? – which, although not intentional, may actually have been rather humorous. I meant to say, this area of *study* is fascinating, but of course it's also true that this *geographical* area is full of interesting features. Hence my pamphlet!

I took a couple steps towards him, and turned sideways so as to squeeze past. But he was still talking:

If I've been looking into the church for whatever reason, I do like to take a turn amongst the trees here. Just, eh, contemplating the works, you know.

I nodded at him, as if understanding perfectly. The works of the forester.

What? Eh! No, of God, God! The works of, eh. . .

Oh him! Of course! With my back pressing into the bushes at the side of the path, I sidled past him, as he stood there looking thoughtful.

We don't see much of you at the kirk these days, do we, Patrick? he said, just as I got by him.

No, you don't, I replied.

He nodded. Not since the funeral service for your, eh, father, if I remember correctly.

Aye, I haven't been since then. Funny that, eh?

He tilted his clasped hands towards me, the forefingers outpointed. You should come along some Sunday, you might get something out of it. We all have our spiritual side.

Aye, I ken. I mean I've been thinking a lot about that kind of stuff recently.

You should *certainly* come along then! You'll find that Jesus has done a lot of this thinking *for you*!

No, that's the. . . I don't want anybody else to do the. . . Oh fuck, I said under my breath.

What was that? said the minister.

Actually, Mr Ritchie, I've been thinking of joining the Free

151

Kirk. I've heard you don't have to put anything in the collection box with them.

He frowned, inclined his body towards me. Indeed? Well well well. That's, eh, remarkable. But the nearest Free Kirk is. . .

Don't worry, Mr Ritchie, I said, taking a backwards step along the path away from him, I was only joking! I took another step, and another.

Ah! Eh. . .very good! he said.

I turned and walked quickly along the old drove road. The darkness was coming down on all sides.

There was a dampness seeping through my ys, and a warmth down there too; no doubt I was also smelling. Just as the woods opened out into a big clearing around the kirk, a rickle of a burn ran alongside the drove road for a few metres before curving back into the mass of trees. I glanced behind me. The minister was nowhere in sight, and his hymnwhistling had faded away several minutes before; probably he was carrying on in the opposite direction.

I knelt down at the side of the track, undid my belt and spaver once more and, grabbing onto a broom bush for support, leant out over the fast-running stream and cupped handfuls of water up over my shrivelled greasy prick. The cold wiped out the overheated sensation immediately, and after a few seconds of sluicing the water up and down, I was feeling fresh and clean. I was wet now, not just damp, but it was a clean wetness, it could dry out of its own accord, no problem.

I jumped up, fastened my breeks, then stepped over the burn and walked through the last few metres of big pines that surrounded the kirk. The building loomed high above in the gloaming, its tall spire black and spindly against the dark blue sky, rising above the tops of even the highest trees, and all around it was a wide white halo of chuckie stones, where folk from outlying farms parked their cars on Sunday mornings. This was also where kids had speedway races and practised handbrake turns on their bikes, sending the chuckies flying and digging down to the dark loamy soil beneath. The elder on duty had to get to work with his rake before the congregation started arriving, covering over the rents and rives in the smooth white circle. Then he'd go inside and ring the bell and rouse the believers of Blackden for their weekly dose of pandrops and platitudes.

As I crunched out of the kirk grounds and turned left to walk the couple hundred metres of special god-blessed pavement along the Aberdeen road back into the village, I became aware of a numbness numbing away between my legs. Through my trouser pocket I gave myself a feel, finding that I'd become severely shrunken and withdrawn, presumably with the cold of my recent dousing. I walked on. At least I was all still there, with no mutilation or scarring in prospect. There's a Kinker man, Billy Rose, who did things just slightly different, and came to a sticky end. . .

Billy's about thirty now, but this would've happened to him when he was about seventeen, and even more clueless. He'd had it off with some poor dame, it seems, and a day or two after he noticed these red pimples appearing on the skin of his cock. Fuck's sake, he thinks, What's this? And he doesn't look again for a couple of days, hoping the things'll just go away. But eventually he risks another keek. Bloody hell! The ends of the pimply bits've gone white, and they're oozing out pus! Fucking hoor, he says to himself, She's given me the pox! I'm smitten! The dreaded totrot!

153

Well, Billy's black affronted, he's over embarrassed to go to the doctor about it – the old boy's a friend of his father's! – so he reckons he'll try a bittie of the old DIY alternative medicine. He gets a half-pint glass, fills it up with bleach, then grits his teeth and plunges in his pimply prick.

Jesus Christ! Just to think about it makes my eyes water!

And Billy is in fucking *agony*, but a man's a man for all that, and he keeps it in for a full three minutes, thinking, This'll kill the pox germs or nothing will! All that day and all of the night he's rolling about in agony, it feels like his goolies are on fire. The next day it's even worse: he can't pish, can't pull his drawers on, can hardly walk. There's nothing else for it, he decides, I'll have to go to the doc or else kill myself. So half an hour later he's in the surgery, breeks round his ankles, and the doctor's saying, Dear oh dear, what have you been doing to yourself? Ah well, says Billy, I think I've caught some kind of a, eh, sex infection. The doc shakes his head. No laddie; I see the remains of a few ordinary spots there – rather like the one or two you have on your face – but they seem to have cleared up of their own accord. What I'm really worried about is the extensive burning over the entire surface of your organ!

I'd reached the square. My feet were hurting with all the day's work and walking, and I couldn't be bothered going all the way home right now. There were already a few cars parked outside the Auld Mill, and I could hear the jukebox playing in the public bar and the sound of drinkers yakking and laughing. That would do for me. Maybe I could even see Shona again, fix up about meeting her later on, tell her I'd been to the Sabbath Stane and. . .seen where the fire was.

I headed for the door of the place, imagining finding myself standing next to Billy Rose at the pub urinal one night. Here Billy,

154

I'd say, Is it true what they say about your scars? Let's have a look at your. . . And round about then I'd have to start picking my teeth out of the pish-bowl.

Wingnut and Jock the Cock were at the dartboard, Jock just lining up to throw. He glanced round as I came in. None of your interruptions tonight, Paddy, he cried, I'm on a roll! You could be witnessing history in the making here!

I stood where I was, and watched. Jock threw.

Oh fuck!

The dart had missed the board completely and bounced back off the wall onto the floor. Jock shuffled his feet around, getting the tips of his toes lined up exactly with the white markings on the rubber distance-mat.

Two arrows in hand, though! he said, then took aim.

Go for it, I said.

He lowered his hand, slowly, slowly, and glared at me. I thought I told you not to interrupt? Please.

I wasn't interrupting, I was encouraging you! What, against the rules to cheer on the players now is it?

Just shut up for once, will you? I grinned at him, and he turned back to the board, aimed, and threw. Yes! That's it! I've done it! History has been. . .

Wingnut turned round from where he had been examining the dart and the board. Just on the wrong side of the wire, he said. Double four now required.

What! Are you sure?

Wingnut nodded, came back to stand out of dart-bouncing range beside me.

This time, said Jock, and threw. The dart flew straight into the centre of the board. Fucking bullseye! he shouted, and punched the air.

That's not what you were needing though, I said.

He walked up to the board, snatched out his two darts and bent to pick the third off the floor. It's still a fucking bullseye though; pretty good fucking throwing if you ask me! I'll get the double four next time, when you're not putting me off.

Wingnut stepped up to the line. I require forty-three, he said, Which could be a seven. . . He threw a seven. . . .and then a double eighteen. He threw a double eighteen. That's it then, he said. Twentytwo nil this week I make it.

Jock went up to the board and poked his nose right against it. Fucking close to the wire that last throw! he said.

Aye, but on the right side, I put in.

Jock sighed, shook his head. It's a great shame, Paddy, cause I was going to say the drinks are on me if I'd fucking won that. As it is, it looks like it's your round, mate.

Hih, I'm not mating with you, Cocky! I started to walk away down the bar. I'm just passing through, I said. I'm not sitting down yet, so. . .you get one in by the time I'm back and I'll even up later.

He muttered something behind my back, but I paid him no heed, and walked on. I stuck my head into the alcove where the pool-table and the jukebox were set up. This got called The Playpen, cause it was where the underagers hung out. Sure enough, there were a couple Kinker lads in, who'd been a few years below me at the school. Aye, aye! I said, and they looked up sharply from their potting.

Aye man, they said, then, Are you needing on? one of them asked. Only we've got money down for another three games yet.

No, you need the practice lads, I'll leave you to it.

As I walked on I could hear balls clicking, and the rumble of one of them rolling into a pocket and down through the innards of the machine. Probably they were ten times better than me, but it's kind of traditional that all underagers should get slagged off whenever possible, just to remind them of their precarious position in the pub. Likewise you have to refer to them as laddies or boys as often as possible. They're not in a position to tell you to fuck off really, especially since Wilson took the place over and started cracking down on the youngsters. Aye, it's hard being young these days: you're not allowed the anaesthetics the adults use.

There was a scattering of other folk, mostly older, along the bar and at the tables. Half of them were staring up at the telly on its shelf, though the football results must've finished an hour before, and anyway, the volume was turned right down. One of the real improvements Wilson had made was to get a telly with a remote control; before, if anyone wanted the channel changed, they had to go and borrow one of the pool cues and push the buttons with that. This led to more than a few scuffles over the years between players unwilling to surrender their stick, or viewers refusing to hand back their channel changer. I nodded to a few of the old guys; most of them had been at the roup earlier on. Mhairi was serving behind the bar again. She looked up as I paused at the end of it.

Aye aye, Paddy. Can I get you something?

Not just yet, ta, I'm just, eh. . . I shrugged towards the door that led to the lobby of the inn. The toilets were off it, as were the doors to the restaurant and the small lounge, and the stairs up to the half-dozen bedrooms, which were supposed to have had twenty grand spent on decorating them over the summer. I'll be back in a sec, I said. I think Jock's getting me one anyway.

Very good.

I went through the swing door, down the three steps, and was in the quiet of the lobby. The thick carpet on the floor soaked up half the noise from the bar, and the rest of it was rinsed away by tinkly piano music coming from speakers high up on the walls. As I stood there, a figure appeared behind the glass door of the restaurant: Gerry Wilson, John's wife. She spent most of her time overseeing the wine and the waiting in the restaurant, which was just as well. Folk got nervous whenever she came into the bar, she seemed so much like a headmistress about to belt a bunch of infants. I think she just disapproved of anybody drinking anything that cost less than ten quid a bottle. She scowled at me through the glass of the door, so I waved to her cheerily. She turned away.

Immediately I stepped sideways and went through the door marked *Staff Only*. Right in front of me was the start of a steep narrow staircase, from the bottom of which floated up the smell of chicken and chips and the sound of banging pans and rattling plates. I went on down, almost without thinking what I was doing, but still feeling excited somehow – my heart starting to thump against my ribs, my mouth suddenly parched – as if I was entering some kind of danger, though of course it wasn't really dangerous, more kind of thrilling that. . .

What the fuck are you doing here! It was John Wilson, coming up round a curve in the stairs towards me, a tray laden with plates of salmon steaks and green sauce in his hands.

Eh, are the bogs down here?

He walked up another step towards me. No, they're fucking not! They're not behind the door with *Private* written on it, funnily enough, no. They're behind the door marked *Gentlemen* for fuck's sake!

I was going to ask him what had happened to his campaign

against staff swearing, but then decided against it, and stepped to the side of the stairs instead, to let him past.

He didn't move. Don't bother standing there, he said. This is a staff area, you've no business being here. Get out!

Oh, sorry, I said, and smiled. It's just, I was needing a bar supper, ken, so I thought I'd come down and order one.

What! I thought you wanted the gents?

Well, aye, and a supper as well. I've heard the food's very good here these days.

Christ, I don't have time to argue. Some folk like to get their meals hot. Get out of my way. . .no: get out of my fucking stair!

I backed up the way. No bother, I said.

If it's no bother, don't make the same mistake again, or this time you really will be barred. I told you last night, your place is upstairs spending money, not down here getting in everybody's way.

I was up against the door. I backed out into the lobby, Wilson coming after me half a second later and steaming straight over towards the restaurant. He paused before going in, straightened himself, and arranged his face to look like a telly gameshow host at prizegiving time.

So what would you recommend thenight? I called out, just as he went to go in.

I'd recommend that you stay well away from my kitchens, or else you'll be walking three miles to your nearest pint from now on!

Do you get chips with that? I said. He'd already disappeared. I headed back to the bar.

*

Dek Duguid had arrived, and was sitting with Jock the Cock and Wingnut at the far end of the bar; all of them were getting to work on fresh pints. I ordered one for myself, seeing as nobody else had, and found an empty stool just along from them: not close enough that I'd have to talk to them unless I really wanted to. Dek was laying off about one of his favourite subjects of the past few months.

The trouble with this place, he said, Is it never fucking changes. It's the same theday as it was last year, and if you stay here you ken it'll be exactly the fucking same in fifty years' time. It's boring! It's dead!

So what's so interesting about the town? said Wingnut. He paused. Everybody looked at him. It's just a load of buildings and a load of folk jammed thegether. He paused again, longer this time, then muttered, Nothing interesting about that.

Dek spluttered into his pint. Nothing interesting? You fucking couthie cunt! That's cause all you're interested in is combine harvesters and enzootic abortions. That's your problem, Wingy. He turned to Jock, who was shaking his head. Here Cocky, he said, You're from the fucking city, fucking Pearly Kings and Queens and all that shite, you ken what I'm talking about, eh?

Jock jumped off his stool. Watch your lip, Derek, he said. Some of my best friends are Pearly Queens.

Oh for fuck's sake.

Jock winked at me as he passed, making for the bog. Dek looked along the bar for back-up.

Hey, Paddy.

What?

What do you think?

What about?

This cunt here, says towns are boring. Least you have the choice to do different stuff there!

Christ, I don't ken, I said. I've never bade in a town.

Aye, me neither, said Dek, But I go into college five days a week and I'm fucking telling you, it's a different world.

I wouldn't ken, I said. You should ask Mhairi, she lived in London. I looked along the bar. She was making bloody marys for someone, a wee bottle of tomato juice in one hand, a squirter of brown sauce in the other. Hey, Mhairi!

She glanced up. Just a second, lads.

Mhairi, hey, tell us about London!

Have patience, Dek, said Wingnut, She's just coming.

I want this settled once and for all, you bastards. He banged his glass down on the bartop. I *ken* about patience. Want to hear what patience is?

Patients is what you get in Foresterhill Hospital, I said quietly, watching Mhairi ringing up the till.

Patience is what the old bastards at my dad's work have, said Dek, Forty years working for Deeside Water Board, and they're still waiting for something interesting to happen. That's the height of fucking patience, and I'm glad I've none of it.

Right, I said, What's the height of pain? Neither of them answered. Okay, I said, It's a fly sliding down a razor-blade using its balls for brakes.

Both of them laughed for half a second, then Mhairi came up. Who's taking down their flies along here then? Come on, give us all some fun.

Hey, Mhairi, said Dek.

What?

Water! said Wingnut.

She stretched along the bar, grabbed the whisky drinkers'

jug sitting there, and slid it along towards him. Anything else?

Aye, listen, said Dek. Tell us about living in the city. I'm trying to explain to Farmer Giles here how it's better than the back of beyond.

God no, Derek, she replied, leaning her elbow on the bar and propping her chin up with her curled fist. The water's much better here than it is in any city.

Christ, stop going on about the water, it's *everything* I mean, life as a whole in the town.

Beasts need good fresh water, said Wingnut, staring into his glass. You'd be surprised how much they get through in a day.

Better not take your nowt to live in London then, I said.

Will you stop going on about the fucking water! cried Dek.

No, but Paddy's right enough, said Mhairi. I was in London, right, worked there for six months, and here's what the state of things was: you could get fancy coffee in miniature cups, you could get freshly-squeezed mango juice in Indian cafes, you could buy Perrier and Highland Spring by the gallon. But if you took a drink out of the tap it was chucking-up time! It tasted like it had been lying in a rusty bucket for six months afore they pumped it into your house.

Dek cradled his head on his two hands, and made sobbing noises. I wish you bastards would stop going on about you-know-what, he said. Christ, it's bad enough having to listen to my dad every night, blethering away about filters and fluoride and foostification. Don't you lot start! All I'm saying is, there must be more to life than tasty fucking water!

Aye, tasty beer, said Mhairi. So were you actually wanting to order anything thenow?

We all shook our heads, except Dek, who just moaned, so she went away to the other end of the bar, where an old farmer had been waving a sharny fiver and loudly clearing his throat for the past ten minutes. Before any of us could say any more, Jock the Cock came in the door from the lobby and strode down towards us.

Ah! he sighed, as he settled onto his stool, circling his backside around on it before easing his weight down. That's a relief boys! A real fucking torpedo!

Fuck's sake, I said, Spare us the details.

Dek looked up. Here, Cocky, you've given me an idea: first thing tomorrow morning, I'm going out to the waterworks, down with my breeks, and crap right in the mains supply for Blackden!

There was a mixture of groans and laughs from the rest of us.

I shook my head. You're sick, Dek, really.

Ach fuck it: it's the only way to react to this fucking dump. Honestly, I'm fucking. . . He slapped his forehead with the palm of his hand. I'll tell you what I heard. I heard that when Wilson was renovating and decorating upstairs – for the tourists he's going to fool into visiting this arsehole of a place – well, up above the lavvy in every room he put a big sign saying, *Leave your comments on Blackden here*, and an arrow pointing down the pan.

Is that right? said Wingnut.

Well if he didn't do it, he should've. Dump on the dump!

Here, boys, said Jock. A joke for you. What's the difference between a bucket of shit and Blackden? Eh? Eh? The bucket!

Christ, I haven't heard that one before. I swallowed the last of my drink and stood off my stool.

Oops! I think I've offended Mr Sensitive, said Jock.

No, I said, Not at all. I'm just away to fucking. . .shake hands with my best friend. But I do have a question for you: Jock, if this place is such a shithole, why did you come here in the first place? Nobody made you.

Ah, the lure of the old black gold drew me, Paddy, that's what it was. Oilderado!

And Dek, if you hate the place so much, why don't you leave? I mean, nobody's making you stay.

He leant off the bar and let his arms fall to his sides, staring at me. Are you going to chuck me out, like?

No, no! That's not the point. The point is, why stay anyplace if you fucking hate it? If I hated someplace, I wouldn't fucking hang around there, I'd be off, I'd be heading somewhere else.

Where would you go? said Wingnut?

Anywhere, anywhere! Like now, I'm fed up of you lot, so I'm heading for the bog. Watch me! Here I go!

I washed some of the work-dirt off my face and hands, had a pish, then rinsed my hands again. I leant on the sides of the sink and stared into the mirror. Who was that guy? How did he get to be such an ugly bastard? And most of all, what the fuck did he have to do with me, that he followed me around everywhere? I turned away from him, and walked out of the bog.

It was quiet in the lobby. I stared at the cigarette machine for a minute, trying to imagine folk's reaction if I ripped it out and installed another machine, selling wee packets of heroin at two quid a time. Their reaction would be: The boy's off his head! It's because his father passed away, obviously. Ever since then he's been a bit. . .you know. But they wouldn't know, they'd be completely wrong, cause my dad never smoked fags, it was always a pipe he had on the go – the fucking healthy way to. . .fuck fuck fuck off.

There was a scratching noise. I listened. A faint scratching noise from somewhere, and a very quiet squeak. Mice? Rats? Surely not, in such a high class establishment. I listened again. It was coming from the *Staff Only* door down to the kitchens. I checked the emptiness of the lobby, went over a couple of steps, and opened it. Something white leapt out, and started rubbing against my leg: the cat from last night. It looked up at me, flashing its one green and one blue eye, purring.

Christ, you're happy to be out of there, I said to it. After you with their cleavers, were they?

The cat gave a wee squeak of a miaow, then took itself off and jumped up the first step of the stairs leading to the bedrooms. It sat down there with its back to me, stretched out one of its hind legs, and started to nibble at the claws on the end of it.

What are you doing, baudrons? I said, and went over to lean on the curved end of the banister.

It would flare open the paw-pads and stick one of the claws into the side of its mouth, gripping with the small white teeth there. Then it would slowly pull its paw away, nibbling with its jaw as it did. After this, it rolled its tongue around its mouth for a few seconds, spat out a bit of pike, and started on the next claw.

That's amazing, I said to it. I've never seen a cat biting its nails before.

It looked up at me, blinked its eyes, then bent back to the manicure. I reached over the banister and scratched it on the back of the head. It started purring again.

Some folk are right easily pleased, I said. Hih! I would be too, if anyone scratched behind my lugs!

It purred loudly.

I walked back along to the bar-door, pausing on the steps there before going in. What if I picked up the cat and flung it through the door of the restaurant? That would give John fucking Wilson something to moan about. A right upset in front of his Gordon Blue diners! But then I thought, he'd probably only strangle the poor beast, and I wouldn't want that.

Here, cat, I said. There's fine comfy beds upstairs, warm too! Go on up!

Mhairi!

Aye?

Pint of heavy please and, eh, I reckon I need to stoke the boilers too.

She watched the beer sputtering out of the tap, and twiddled the nozzle a bit. Eh?

Any chance of some grub?

Grub? Just tell me what you want. The bar menu's beside the ice there.

Oh aye. I looked at the list of food. The cheapest thing these days was one-fifty, and that was just a cheese toastie.

Here's your pint. Made up your mind?

I closed the menu. Aye, seafood pie, please. Will I pay now?

Can do: six pounds exactly.

She took my money and stuck it away; from down the side of the till she drew a small pad, wrote my order on it, and tore it off. Then she lifted the flap at the end of the bar and ducked out and away through the door into the lobby.

I picked up my pint, took a sup, and went to sit at an empty table; I couldn't be bothered mixing it with Dek the city slicker any more thenight. But thirty seconds later someone walked up and stood beside my table, bumping it with their thighs, and I looked up and it was Dek.

Just thought I'd tell you I'm fucking off now, he said.

Oh aye?

Aye. He sniffed.

What's it to me?

Well, just to let you know: I'm away to watch American football on the satellite. Got a bit of a carry-out and that. He swung his carrierful of cans so they banged against my knees under the table.

Very good, I said. Enjoy yourself.

He sniffed again. Aye, I will. But it's just to let you know: I mean usually I'd ask you to come along, ken, and I didn't want you to get back from the bog and find me gone and think I'd forgotten about you.

So what are you saying, Dek? Are you asking me to come along or not?

Nah, I'm not asking you. I've remembered you and I'm not asking you, that's the fucking point.

Fuck's sake. I shook my head. Nice of you to tell me, you miserable bastard.

I'm just being straight with you, Paddy. I don't want you back at my place any more.

So who are you wanting back then? Wingnut? Jock the Cock? Or are you just not bothering with mates at all these days?

He curled his top lip. I've got friends, he said, Don't you worry. Plenty of friends. Aye, and not sad old cunts like Jock the Cockless either. Or Wingnut with his stink of cows and his face like a cow's and his talk of cows and his fingers like cows' tits. And his brain the size of a fucking cow's. I've had it up to here with the lot of you. I'm fucking *off*. You're welcome to this shithole, it's all you're fit for.

I stood up so I was facing him. Here, Dek, mind I was saying the other day I wouldn't lash out till I had a fucking good reason for it?

What about it?

Well unless I'm very much misfuckingstaken, you just gave me one. How about. . .

Hi, lads, how are you doing? It was Mhairi, stepping in between us. I was just down in the kitchens, Paddy, and Shona says the seafood pie's off thenight – there's been a run on it or something – so I told her haddock and chips instead, okay? I thought that was probably the closest. So that'll just be five minutes, she's a fast wee worker, Shona. Okay? Oh, and another thing: the fish is fifty p cheaper, and I can't really take the money back out of the till once it's rung up, ken, so I just brought you this over instead. Okay? Byyyeee.

She zipped off amongst the tables, collecting empty glasses and crisp packets. On the table in front of me was a new half-pint of heavy. Standing beside me was. . .nobody. Dek had buggered off. I sat down, took a big drink of my original pint, then poured the new half into the space I'd made. The two glasses tinkled together as I poured. My hand was shaking.

Thank fuck it hadn't come to a scrap. I'd been wrong, I hadn't had a good enough reason to hit Dek. Even as I was saying to him that I had, I was thinking to myself that I hadn't. The same old story as per always. Maybe it was just that my brain moved too quick or something. If it'd taken me five minutes to realise that I hadn't a good enough reason, it would've been too late, it would all've been over: I'd've fucking chinned the bastard. But no, it hadn't worked out like that, my knuckles remained unskinned. And was that a bad thing? No. Except that now I had a fightful of adrenalin charging through my veins and brain, and nothing to do with it. My hands were jittering, my feet tapping away on the floor of their own accord, and my thoughts were spinning and wobbling like a bird-scare in a gale.

I jumped to my feet again, grabbed my pint, and walked back to the end of the bar where Jock and Wingnut were still sitting, now with Bri on my old stool, and the mannie Ronaldson on Dek's. He was facing away, though, his elbows resting on the bar behind him, as he watched Roosty and another farmer attacking the dartboard.

Aye aye, man, said Bri.

Aye, Bri, I said. What like?

Not bad. Just got here, like.

Oh aye? Needing a drink? I reckon I owe you one from last night.

Well. . .

That's good of you, Paddy, said Jock the Cock. Same again, if you please – and for Wingy as well, I should think.

I leaned over the bar at the side of Bri's stool; he walked it along slightly so I could get in. Mhairi! When you're ready! Lager for Bri and the same again for these characters.

Okay, right with you.

I turned back to Bri. Here, guess who I saw theday.

Dek Duguid in a roose.

Aye, well I did see him, but it wasn't him I was meaning. Geronimo and Tonto!

Bri looked at me for a second, then burst out in a grin. Ha! Aye! Christ, you don't see them around much these days. They're still on the go though?

Here, Jock came in, Who the fuck are you talking about?

Hih, well, it's these two guys that bide up on the side of the Ben. They live in a fucking wigwam, Cocky!

Bollocks!

169

It's true. Eh, Wingnut? Wingnut looked into his pint, went red in the lugs. And here's another one to bamboozle you, Jock, I went on. I also just met the mannie Arse, do you ken him?

No I don't.

Aye you do, said Bri, and laughed.

I think I'd remember a name like that.

Ah, but only if you kent the code!

Come on then, Paddy, assuming it's not yourself we're talking about here, who's this Arse?

Hih. It's the Reverend Robert Ritchie. Three Rs, you see: Arse! I laughed, and so did Bri and Wingnut. After making-on not to find it funny for a minute, Jock joined in.

See what you missed by not being a loon here? said Bri.

All sorts of bollocks by the sounds of it!

Mhairi arrived in front of me, plonked down a plate, and dashed away to the Murphy's pump, which she'd left running.

Great, I said. Fish and chips. Shame about the unnecessary salad! Jock immediately leant over and started dragging off a big bit of lettuce. I went for his fingers with my fork. But that doesn't mean you can nick it, you cunt! He laughed. I forked up the lettuce and crammed it into my gob, then started on the haddock. It's funny, I said, chewing, But some names just fit folk perfect. Like you're called Jock the Cock, and you're a complete cunt. . .the names fit, see? He gave me the finger, but the others grinned. You were a bit slow on the uptake about these things, eh? Mind when you first came here and you started calling everybody Jock? I was just about ten at the time, but I mind folk saying, Who's this mad cockney going about calling everybody Jock? Does he not ken we're all Scottish around here? He's not going to get far if he calls everyone with a Scottish accent Jock!

Whoo! Wingnut put back his head and hooted.

Okay, okay, very funny. Aye, that rebounded on me, didn't it, said Jock. And here's the worst of it: when I go south to see the old dear and my brothers and that, they all think I've got a Scotch accent! They all call me fucking Jock! And I go, Aye, I mean, *Yes*, what is it? Ha! I think they're saying my name!

A couple guys next to us bought half-bottles to carry out and left the pub. I forked up a big mouthful of chips and batter, nudging my empty glass with my elbow as I lifted it. Whoops! I cried. That was nearly my glass over there! Good job it's empty, eh Bri?

My round already is it? he said, grinning.

No, it's mine, said Wingnut, and got his wallet out.

Jock waved a hand in front of his face. Christ! Where's all these moths coming from?

We all laughed, but Bri seemed to be straining a bit to manage it: he could only ever take so much of Jock. Right enough, I was the same. I'd hardly ever talked to him for this long before. Dek was always the guy I had long hours of yapping with, ever since we were kids. We were always blabbing about what we'd do when we grew up, all the jobs we'd have, the cars we were going to drive, the women we were going to take out in the cars, the drinks we were going to get them drunk on – and ourselves too! We were wrong on just about all our predictions, except Dek did manage to do the drinking and driving bit for a wee while – and now we couldn't thole each other's company long enough to come up with any new ones. So that was one more way I wasn't going to work out what lay in the future.

Finished? It was Mhairi, reaching to take away my empty plate.

Eh, aye, that was great. Complimentaries to the chef! She left, and I turned to the lads. Here, I never finished what I was saying earlier. . .

What, the bit about you owing me a fiver? said Jock.

No, listen. Mind I said I met in with the minister?

Arse, you mean? Jock grinned. See, I'm learning!

Aye, well, he was acting a bittie strange, I thought.

How? said Bri.

I met him in the woods behind the kirk. . .

Oh aye! Arse-man! Say no more!

Aye, Jock, I was taking a shortcut back from my work actually. Anyway, there he was, wandering about amongst the trees down by the old Sabbath Stane. Ken where I'm at, Bri?

He nodded. Aye, we did that at the school, I think. That was where the witches' coven used to meet, eh?

That's the place. And that's the strange thing, right. Ritchie lets on to me that he was hanging about down there as well a couple weeks ago. And you ken what a couple weeks ago was? I leant towards them, and said quietly, Halloween.

So?

So, just last night, Shona Findlay was telling me she'd seen lights and stuff dancing about in the Kirk Woods in the middle of Halloween night. Fucking weird or what?

So are you saying, said Bri, That you reckon Arse is some kind of a witch or something?

I looked over my shoulders to make sure nobody was nebbing in. I'm not saying anything. I'm asking you: do you think he could be? Or anybody hereabouts might be? I mean, have you seen anything like that going on?

They all thought for a few seconds, taking the chance to drink at the same time.

Well, said Jock.

Aye?

Well, I'm not saying I've seen anything myself, but Bobby

172

Halcro was complaining the other night cause he was looking for Shona's car, and it had just. . .completely. . .disappeared!

Och, come on!

No, but listen, Jock went on, That Shona's a bit of alright, eh? I wouldn't mind doing a bit of the old black magic with her! A bit of the old voo-doo!

Christ, shut up!

What? You telling me to shut up?

If you're not going to take it fucking seriously.

Come on, said Bri, Are you saying you're serious about this witch shite?

I looked round the three of them over the top of my pint glass. I swallowed. Nah, I'm having you on! Broomsticks and fucking bedknobs? In Blackden? Hih! I had you going though!

Here, said Wingnut, I've just thought of this, listen. What do you call a drunk pigeon?

Is this a joke? said Jock.

Aye. It's a joke. I just made it up!

What was the start again? I said.

It was, What do you call a pigeon that's drunk?

That's not very funny, said Bri.

No, listen. I haven't told you the end yet.

Oh aye. Right from the top, Wingy!

Right. What do you call a drunk pigeon?

I don't know, said Bri. What do you call a drunk pigeon?

Wingnut looked at each of us in turn, then burst out, A foo-doo! Get it? A foo-doo!

In the time it took to drink another pint, the pub half-emptied. Roosty had finished his darts, come up to buy a bottle of voddy, and left. His old man was still sitting at the end of the bar, though, still facing out the way; it turned out he hadn't been watching the dartboard at all, he was looking through into The Playpen, where a group of quines had taken over the pool. Every time one of them leant over the table he'd lick his lips at the tightness of her jeans or the shortness of her skirt. It was the kind of thing that made you want to bring a shovel down on his bald head, like a teaspoon smashing open a boiled egg.

Oi, Howbrae.

He jumped slightly, and turned round towards me. What, loon?

Where's Roosty off till? Not like him to leave afore closing time.

He's away up to the curling.

Is the curling on, is it? Bri broke in.

Aye, said the mannie Ronaldson. He's had his stones in the car all week on the off-chance. He turned to look away from us again. I had the feeling he was being a bit shifty towards me, but I could've been imagining it.

Fucking magic! said Bri. I was thinking we must be just about there, with this long spell of frosts. Let's go! He swallowed the last mouthful of his drink, jumped off his stool, and pulled on his jacket.

What's this? said Jock. Where are you going?

Curling, said Bri, feeling in his pockets. Coming?

Fuck that for a game of soldiers! It's cold enough walking home, never mind standing around on a slab of ice for hours!

Bri shrugged. Wingnut?

Nah. . .

Ah weil, just you and me then, Paddy.

Eh. . .looks like it. I stood up. Okay.

Shit! I'm out of siller. Fuck! How can you go to the curling without a nip in your pocket to warm you?

Don't fash, I said. I'll get some. I've got a bit of whisky-money set aside, as it happens.

I bought a half-bottle of Grouse, fitted it into the inside pocket of my jacket, and we left.

We walked through the crossroads and on out the Kincardine O'Corse road, the hall on our left, the primary school on our right. I nodded over towards it.

Mind in that playground in winter? When it froze up we'd have great slidies the whole length of the boys' section. The dominie was always out shouting at us that we'd fall and crack our heads open!

Bri laughed. Aye, and the old bastard would send out George the jannie afore playtime to spread salt on the thing and melt it.

But we'd just make another one right alongside it. And there *was* always somebody split their head!

We stepped off the pavement and walked along the road for a while, then turned off up the wynd to the pleasure park. There were no streetlamps on here, and the trees on each side blocked out half the light of the stars and the moon. We slowed down, our feet slipping a little on the leaves frosted to the tarmac.

That aye used to give me the shivers, I said. Christ!

What? Cold days?

No, the idea of somebody's head getting split open. I used to hate it when the dominie or my folks or anyone said that, cause I could just imagine it, ken. I could just imagine speeding along that slide, then SKITE, my feet go out from under me and CRACK my head hits the playground concrete. Then it would split open, my head, come right into two pieces, like a chocolate easter egg with all the sweeties spilling out the middle. I could just see the two halves of my head splitting apart and falling to each side! Jesus! And there'd be me, my brains starting to spill out, and I'd have to hold the two halves of my head, one in each hand, and cram the brains in with my thumbs, and I'd have to go running along to the teachers' staffroom to get a bit of sellotape to wrap around my head to hold it all together.

Bri was laughing.

What? I said. Did you have the same thing too?

You're joking! he said. I was just thinking how you were always a weird bastard, even when you were fucking seven!

I thought about this for a minute. I wasn't weird, I said. I just believed everybody too much. Like if the dominie said my head would split open, I really thought my head would split open. If somebody told me to keep my eyes peeled, I used to get the grue thinking of peeling the skin off my eyes like off of grapes or something.

Like I said, you were always weird.

We were passing the gate to the pleasure park. The road wound on round the end then the far side of it, before reaching the bowling green with the curling rink next to it. I started to turn into the park.

Where are you going? said Bri. You can't get in that way.

Fuck it, I said. We'll just nip across the pitch then in under the fence. I'm not paying a pound to get in the front gate! Christ, we're only watching, not playing. It's not like we're going to wear away the ice with our eyes or anything.

But I might want to play a few ends. . .

Well, here's the beauty of the system: you can pay once we're in if you want to, only nobody fucking has to!

We strode in through the park gate and onto the pitch. The

frosted grass crackled as we walked over it, and a limey smell worked its way into my nostrils. New markings down, I said. Must be a match themorn.

Us versus the Civil Service Strollers. Fancy coming along? Should be a laugh – there was five goals and three red cards last time we played them.

What I want to know, I said after a few moments, Is how come the team has to be called Blackden United? I mean there's only about two hundred folk in the place!

Ach, it's just a name.

The moonlight was shining down on the darkness of the grass. We crossed into the centre circle, then I stopped. Hold on a minute, I said, and took down my spaver and splattered the centre-spot with a few pints of heavy-piss.

Bullseye, said Bri.

But why that name do you think? Did there used to be a Blackden Rovers and a Blackden Academicals and one day they got together and decided they should be United?

You're talking shite again, Paddy.

I zipped up, wiped my hands on the legs of my breeks. Ken this, I reckon they should start a five-a-side team and call it Blackden Divided. I'd play for a team with that name.

Bri laughed. No team would have you, you bastard!

Hih. You're right. At one time that would've worried me, but not now. Now I just think, Three cheers for me! Come on you Hunter!

Ha!

We stopped talking and just walked, out of the centre circle and on across the pitch towards the corner, where a row of monkey puzzle trees marked the edge of the pleasure park. Beyond that there was a slight rise in the ground, then the bowling green and the curling. The thing hadn't really been built as a rink, it was really meant to be a tennis court, but after it'd flooded every autumn and frozen every winter about five years on the trot, folk realised that it'd be a lot handier for bonspiels than trailing away up to the pond in the grounds of Corse House. Plus with the water being only a foot deep on the tennis, it froze a lot quicker than the pond, which was deep enough for fish and ducks and drowning. My granda told me all about this, cause he'd been a young lad when they first started curling here; back in the twenties, I suppose

We walked under the thick jaggy branches of the monkey puzzles, up the rise beyond, then stopped, dazzled, to look down at the rink.

It seemed at first that the trees around the rink were blazing, but after a second you could make out that the light was bright and steady and white. Somebody had been up half a dozen of them and hung some kind of floodlights, two in each tree. There were lights at the corner, then others in the middle of each long side, and they were all pointing in the way and down, so the ice blazed white in the dark night. The brightness of the rink made the surrounding trees and grass look even darker than they were anyway; after thirty seconds of staring, my brain was starting to tell me that my eyes were seeing a white shining rectangle floating through black space.

I blinked a few times. Will we go down?

Hold on a minutie, I'm needing to see who's all there.

Bits of conversation were drifting up to us from the various small groups of folk standing about the ice, passing round hip-flasks and half-bottles and getting their stones out of zipper bags. Every few seconds someone would shout over to one of the other groups, or there would be a whistly scratching noise as somebody went skiting across the ice, testing it out or going to greet a new arrival. At one end, a proper game had already started. There was a howl of laughter from one of the groups of folk on the next rink along from that, like a hound throwing back its head and letting rip.

Oh fuck, said Bri, My father's here. I was hoping he wouldn't've heard about it.

You haven't fallen out with your folks, have you?

Nah nah, we get on fine. It's just, come the wee hours he'll be sliding about down there absolutely mankit, and everybody'll be expecting me to carry him home. Including him. He sighed. Only one thing for it. . .

. What's that?

Give us the Grouse and I'll show you.

I handed him the bottle and he broke the seal, then there was a glugging sound like a calfie cowking on a lump of neep: Brian getting wired in to the whisky. After a minute he lowered the bottle from his mouth, gasped for air, then said to me in a husky voice, See, if I'm even pisseder than him, I *can't* carry him home! Someone else'll have to carry the both of us! He nudged the bottle against my elbow. But here, have some yourself – it's cold work standing about thenight.

I looked, caught a glint from the bottle, and reached for it. But suddenly I didn't feel like drinking. I didn't want anybody carrying me anywhere. I passed the bottle back to Bri. We should go down, I said.

Aye, I suppose. Here, what've you been doing with this? Sniffing it just?

Ach. . .you keep a hold of it, Bri, have as much as you like. I'm off the fucking yoosky boosky thenight.

Jesus. Thanks, Paddy. Are you sure though? I'll pay you back.

Forget it. That was just a bit of cash I came into, I wasn't expecting it. Whisky was the thing to get with it.

Still. . .

Fuck it, I said. Let's get down to the ice afore summer comes and it melts.

We started down the slope through dead bracken and stiff frozen grass, and ducked through the same gap in the mesh fence that we'd been using since we were kids. We paused there, under one of the floodlighting trees. There were two car batteries lying against the trunk, and cables leading up into the branches.

I'm going to have a word with my dad, said Bri, See if I can get a loan of his stones for a few ends later on. Fancy it yourself?

Another couple games had started up. I watched the players and their stones sliding about at high speed. Christ, you're not getting me out on that ice, I said. I'd only fall and split my head open.

Mr Brindle!

He lowered the big camera down from in front of his face. Yes?

It's me, Paddy.

I don't know any Paddys.

Patrick Hunter, I work for Murray Marts. Mind, we were talking this afternoon.

Ah, yes, of course. Well. . .

Well I just arrived, like, and I saw you standing up at the end here, and I wanted to talk to you, ken, I wanted to. . .

Silence! he cried, and raised the camera again. I'm working, he said, and, bending slightly at the knees, aimed out across the ice and clicked, whirred, clicked, whirred.

What are you. . .

Shh!

I looked out past his shoulder which, even with him stooping, was still level with my forehead. Four playing areas had been marked out. At one side of the rink, circular targets a few metres across were scored into the ice, drilled holes marking the bullseyes; at the other side, wooden foot-boards had been fixed in hacks in the frozen surface. Different knots of folk were gathered on the ice around the playing areas – the curlers – and many more were spectating from the grass banks around the rink. Some of these, waiting their turn to play, had curling stones at their feet. Others were just watching, and shouting out encouragement and criticism and sure-fire advice.

Brindle clicked and whirred a few more times, occasionally muttering things under his breath, and giving little grunts of excitement. He seemed to be concentrating on the game closest to us; the three other games were all-male affairs, but the nearest one was between two teams of women.

I watched as a woman in a red padded jacket stepped up to the hack-board, brushed the bottom of the stone with the palm of her hand, then crouched into position. She tilted her head to aim, rocked back on one foot, and bounced forward, her throwing arm outstretched with the stone at the end of it. The woman and the stone moved forward together for a few seconds, then slowly her fingers loosened from round the stone's handle, and it glided onwards by itself as she gradually came to a stop. Two of the thrower's team-mates skidded along just to the side of the stone, long-handled brushes held at the ready. For five seconds the players were silent, though the stone made a growling sound as it rumbled across the ice; then, as it started to slow down a good few metres short of the target circles, the thrower suddenly yelled out, SWEEP! SWEEP GIRLS, SWEEP! Her two team-mates immediately set their brushes to the ice in front of the stone and scrubbed at a fantastic rate; they looked like a speeded-up film from a floor-cleaner ad. Hurry girls, hurry! shouted the thrower, rising up slightly from her crouch at last, and pushing herself down the ice to follow the action. Then, STOP! she called. They stopped, leant back, glanced behind them at the circles, where four stones were already lying. Just over, just over! yelled the thrower suddenly, and one of the brushers swept like mad for another three seconds, causing the stone to veer slightly, missing another stone that was lying directly in its path on the edge of the outermost circle. Instead it clipped the edge of a third one, sending it inching towards the centre of the target. Yes! shouted the thrower, and the brushers and some of the spectators gave a few claps.

Brindle jumped up straight and cried, Right to the tee! Well done, Marjorie! And the thrower did a mock curtsey as she scooted over the ice to have a look at the arrangement of the stones.

I looked at Brindle. Here, is that your. . .

That's my wife, Marjorie, he said, and clicked a stud, fastening a leather case around his camera.

She's a curler?

Evidently. He waved to her, down at the target, already planning the next shot with her team-mates.

She's good!

Southern Ladies Champion three years running.

That's amazing.

Before we were married. In fact, quite a lot of our courtship was prosecuted on sheets of ice on cold dark nights! Nowadays she just plays occasionally, for pleasure. But I've amassed quite a collection of photographs of her and her compeers in action. In fact, I've been thinking of selecting some of them as illustrations for a calendar. I believe there'd be quite a market for such an item in Canada as well as here. Curly Girlies, I might call it. What do you think?

The way he said it, without any rs, it sounded like Kelly Gellies, that's what I thought. But I said, Not bad, but I bet you could improve on it, Mr Brindle. How about, eh, Skirling Girlies Birl and Swirl While Curling?

Skelly Gellies. . . Hm, perhaps, Patrick, perhaps. You certainly do have a way with. . .

Aye, that's what I want to talk to you about, actually, I said. That job you were offering me, the one for the mottoes and the mucking and that.

Shh! He flung up a hand in front of my mouth, and darted his eyes all around the rink, including a good peer out into the trees behind us. You never know who's going to be listening, he said, quietly.

I doubt anyone here's very interested, Mr Brindle.

Don't you believe it, boy. When word of my new HQ up at Goodman's Croft gets out, it'll become a target for industrial-espionage by every greeting-card and novelty-towel manufac-turer in the country. I'm having full security equipment installed next week. And a dog.

I spread my hands. But you know I'm not a spy, Mr Brindle.

Well, I can't be too sure, can I? I mean you didn't exactly leap at the opportunity to take up my offer of a career-opening this afternoon. Could that be because you're already in the pay of one of my competitors? Sweetheart's of Dundee, perhaps?

What? Nah! I laughed, shaking my head.

Are you laughing at me, boy? He took a step towards me,

glowering. I seem to hear a lot of laughter as I go about my business in Blackden, but I can never see anything funny.

I'm not laughing, I said, straightening my face.

Wise, he said. Otherwise I might begin to have doubts about your suitability for my organisation.

Good.

Good?

Aye, very good. It's good you beginning to have doubts.

I was getting cold standing there, so I took a few steps off to one side, swung my hands against my ribs a couple times, and stomped my feet up and down. Then I walked back towards Brindle. But I didn't like the look of him, so I kept on walking, right past him.

Where are you going, Hunter? he said.

Good question! I walked on a few steps further till I was standing at the very edge of the rink, and gazed out at the players and stones whizzing about the ice, and the spectators grouped on the slopes all around. The thing is, Mr Brindle, I said over my shoulder, I saw you standing here, so I thought I'd take the opportunity to tell you something: I want nothing to do with you or your company. Never. I don't want your job. Wouldn't want it in a million years.

He came up beside me, nodding slowly. I see, he said, then fell silent, staring out over the curling. Eventually he sighed and said in a tired voice, So you have been recruited by one of my rivals.

I let out a hoot of laughter. Fuck's sake! No! I wouldn't work for them in a million years either!

Humh. I must say I find that hard to believe. I mean I just don't understand it. Why would anyone in their right mind turn down such an offer?

Why? Why? Because. . . I can't take the job because. . . I

184

scanned the rink, looking for a reason for him. Then I found one: my granda standing by himself up at the far end, watching the game there. I'm leaving, I said, and started walking away from Brindle.

You're leaving Blackden? he said after me.

No! I said, then added, Aye, aye, that's it.

I reckon these are the best curlers here thenight, he said. I've been watching since the start, and both teams've been playing real clever stuff.

I've been here since near the start as well, I said, But there was a bit of business I had to get sorted, so. . .

The freezing air was full of players shouting instructions at each other, spectators cheering or laughing or clapping, and underneath it all the constant hollow rumbling of the stones sliding along the ice, and the sharp CLACKs as they smacked into each other.

What? said my granda.

Noisy business, eh!

The roaring game, they call it, Paddy. Though whether it's the players or the rocks that roar the loudest I've never been siccar!

We watched the play for a few minutes.

Hey, Granda, the loon that just threw, I ken him, he's a friend of mine.

Is that a Ronaldson?

Aye, Roosty, from Howbrae. Is he good? He looked good to me.

Ah well, Paddy, the end result was good, but it took an awful lot of effort to get there. You shouldn't have to strain, ken, you're not wrestling. It should be a graceful thing between you and the stone and the ice. But he's not bad for a youngster, I'll give him that.

Roosty had moved up to the target, and was standing with his team-mates, all of them pointing out angles of attack to each other, moving their hands and the heads of their brushes over the rink to show possible movements of the stones. The opposing team was just about to play.

Right now, Willie, shouted a middle-aged man from the centre of the circles.

Aye skip? said the player waiting to throw.

I want you to take out that guard at the front of the house, said the skip. Give it a good bit of weight and we'll maybe strike out their winner as well.

He slid back through the stones to the edge of the rink, and the two brushers stood at the ready halfway down. The thrower got a grip on the board, crouched, then sprang forward and released the stone. It roared over the ice.

Leave it, leave it! shouted the skip.

The two sweepers skidded along, their brushes twitching in their hands but never touching the surface of the rink.

Suddenly the stone gave a slight jouk, and started curving out to one side.

SWEEP! yelled the thrower, and the skip shouted as well: Robbie, sweep! Hurry! Hurry!

One of the sweepers dived in with his brush, flew at the ice with it, his arms working like pistons, but the stone continued to curl slightly out of line, and it passed right by the guard-stone it'd been aimed at and into the house. Roosty immediately moved forward and started brushing hard in front of the stone, and the thing sped right on, missing all the other stones and dunting into the grass verge at the back.

The skip bent over double with his head in his hands for a second, then straightened up again. That was a lovely bit of fresh air, he said to the thrower, who was walking towards him, shrugging. Never mind, Willie, never mind. . .

The oldest man in Roosty's team took a last look at the layout of the stones in the target area, and moved away down the ice, pausing about halfway down and bending to pick something up from the surface. He turned back to the other players.

Somebody's shedding a hell of a lot of hairs, he said. Have a look, eh lads?

Right-o skip. The others checked their brushes.

I thought he meant somebody was going bald, I said.

Ho! My granda half turned to me. But watch this, Paddy, this'll be this team's last throw this end. They'd better put another guard in the twelve-foot circle there, or the other skip'll draw in through that gap and take their winner right out. I've seen him do it twice thenight already!

The stone was launched, the thrower sliding after it almost all the way down the rink without rising from his crouch. There was a fierce bit of sweeping at the last moment, and the stone glided up smoothly and came to a rest, just kissing the one at the centre spot.

Good play, said my granda, and clapped. Cracking an egg, you call that, Paddy. There's two to knock out in front of the tee now.

The opposition's skip was already lining up to throw.

Go for it, Dovie! somebody shouted beside me, and there were a few cheers from other of the folk watching.

He showed no sign of hearing them, but stepped up to the hack, crouched down, and sent the stone sailing down the ice, circling slowly as it went. The handle on top pointed first back the way, then sideways, then finally right round to the front and back again as the stone spun slowly round, curving in a shallow arc towards the house. The skip stood up and ran after it. Draw it round, Robbie, draw it round! he shouted, and there was a burst of sweeping. The stone roared past the front guard, missing it by millimetres, and went CRACK into the winner and the other stone lying up against it.

He's hit the double! said my granda, and cries went up all around.

All three stones were now in movement, rolling slowly outwards away from the tee. All the brushers dived into action, working like crazy at the other side's stones to get them moving as far from the centre as possible. There were shouts of, Hurry lads, hurry! from both skips, and various whoops and shouts from the spectators. Some of the players from the next rink even glanced over for a second, before turning back to their own game.

Then, after a last frenzy of sweeping from Roosty in front of a seemingly stationary stone, the play was over. All the curlers crowded round the house, stepping carefully so as not to nudge the stones, and nearby spectators walked onto the ice too, craning their necks to have a look at the closeness of the final result. A great discussion started up, several dozen folk chipping in their opinion simultaneously.

We can't miss this, I said, and stepped out onto the rink, but my granda was already away, taking firm treads towards the bunch of players and spectators.

Well this red one's out of it, somebody was saying as I reached the house. See, it's biting the eight-footer; none of the others is biting the line.

The two skips moved round to look at the stone in question.

What do you reckon? said Roosty's skip.

He's right, said the other.

Roosty's skip gave the stone a gentle kick, and it rumbled away, two spectators stepping aside to let it roll clean through onto the open ice. I looked back into the centre of the circle. The skips were down on their hunkers by the tee, conferring.

Anybody got a tape-measure? somebody in the crowd said, and there was laughter. Just at that second, the skips stood up.

Aye, it's close, said Roosty's skip.

But I reckon it's your end, said the other, and went to shake hands. Immediately there was a great cheer from Roosty and his team-mates, and most of the spectators. Six-four! somebody cried. It's all over! Good play all round though, somebody else said, Great game... Folk were slapping each other on the back and hugging and passing around bottles of whisky. All of a sudden it was like The Bells at Hogmanay.

I eased myself back out of the crowd, and took a few steps away towards the empty end of the playing-area. I was starting to feel the cold. Unlike most folk, who'd come prepared for a long stand in the open air, I'd only my leather jacket on, no big coat or hat or gloves. I swung my arms about me a couple of times and clapped my hands together, breathing out great clouds of steam that showed for an instant in the glare of the floodlights then vanished. I stamped my feet, glancing across the rink to where the three other games were still in progress, with stones roaring along, brushers and throwers chasing after them, and spectators applauding and catcalling. Then I stubbed my toe on something, my feet slipped from under me, and I went sprawling onto the ice. In an instant I was up, looking around me, whistling a bit of nothing; but it was okay, no one was even looking in my direction. The beamer that had been rising to my cheeks subsided. Only then did I notice that I'd taken a right dunt on the tail of my spine, and it was throbbing away nastily. I gave it a rub. At least nobody had seen me go sklite.

I looked around. A metre away a curling stone was sitting by itself, the one that had been biting the eight-foot line half a minute before. I carefully stepped over, wrapped my fingers round the rubber grip on its handle, and made to lift. It was much heavier than I'd thought, and I was almost thrown off balance and onto my backside again. Once recovered, I placed my feet flat on the ice, one on each side of the stone, and bent down to grab it again. This time I used the weight of the thing to hold me down on the slippery surface, and I swung it back and forth between my legs, just a couple centimetres above the ice.

Still holding the stone in the air, I took a few steps towards the hack-board; then I thought to let it rest on the ice again, and slid it forward a few more steps. I stopped and turned, my hand on the grip, closed one eye, and lined up the stone with the steer of folk still standing about laughing and talking and drinking in the target area. If I threw the thing hard enough, and my aim was true, the whole lot of them would go flying down like skittles. I swung the stone back and forward; a long way back and a long way forward, and. . .at the last second didn't let it go, but kept a tight grasp, the momentum of the brute almost sucking my arm out of its socket as I held on. Then I released the stone, it sat on the ice in front of me, and I put a hand inside my jacket to rub my raxed shoulder: I seemed set on injuring myself thenight. . .

You'll not get far unless you let the fucking thing go, somebody said behind me, and laughed.

I turned. It was Bri.

You have to let the fuckers go, he said again, and sat down on the ice. It looked like he'd polished off most or all of my Grouse.

Aye man, I said. Fine night for it.

Do you want a tip, Paddy? Do you? You have to let go of the fuckers, or you'll never get near where you're aiming. Simple as that. Fucking chuck them away!

How about you, I said. Did you get a game? There was a good one here. Well, I just came in at the end of it, like, but Roosty Ronaldson's team won: six ends to four. He's good, Roosty.

I lost, said Bri. Fucking lost. To my own dad! He shook his head. See this ice? It's fucking shite! Feel it, feel it!

From where he was sitting, he reached out and grabbed my wrist, pulled it down towards the ice. I went with it, and laid my palm flat out on the surface. It felt cold, and wet, and also slightly grainy.

See? he said.

Eh, it's kind of rough.

It's hell of a dauchie! he cried. And full of biases as well: fucking keen here, dull there. . .useless!

Make things hard does it?

You can tell just by looking at it! Fucking useless white shite! It should be black, Paddy, fucking so clear you can see the tennis markings through it. But this has been fucking frozen and thawed and frozen and rained on and fucking. . .it's a fucking. . . . He chapped the ice with his knuckles. Fucking useless!

Here, you won't believe this, Bri. . . I started.

It's drawing like fucking crazy up at the far end, where the fucking quines've been playing all night, but down here you can't get a curl off it at all. Inbetween it's all over the fucking shop!

Aye, but down with the women, did you see who was. . .

Help me up will you? Bri held his hands out to me. I can't get fucking up! He moved his feet about on the ice, but he couldn't get them to grip at all, he was just slithering about. I'll be alright once I get in the car, he said.

I grabbed hold of one of his arms at the elbow, and pulled. He didn't rise at all, just slid across the ice towards me on his arse, then fell back and banged his head. He started laughing. I grabbed both his arms this time, pulled him round on his back till his feet were jammed against mine, and yanked. He sagged upwards and staggered onto his feet, slumping against me for a second, then pushed himself away and stood, swaying slightly, one arm resting on my shoulder. I don't think you should be driving, I said. Remember Dek.

Aye, but be sensible: I can hardly *walk* all the way home like this, can I? He started laughing again. Here, maybe some lucky lady'll drive me. He paused for a moment, then shouted, LUCK! LUCK! Luck be a lady tonight. . . After a few seconds I realised he was singing.

Let's go and have a seat over here, I said, and steered the two of us off towards the grass bank. Bri continued shouting about luck and ladies for a bit, then started speaking again. It took me a while to work out what he was on about.

Fucking Marjorie last night man, I'm telling you: out of this fucking world, Paddy. Beautiful, befuckingutiful! Swept off my fucking feet! Last night and thenight, eh? Ha! Fucking Marjorie Brindle. . . What are you doing here? I says. Local culture, she says, Want to see local culture.

We reached the edge of the rink. I turned us round in a half-circle so we were back-on to the grass, then sat us down. Aye, I said, But did you not see. . .

Christ, I'll show you culture, I says. Wey-hey! I'll fucking show her! But. . . He held up a finger. If I'd kent this was on thenight, I'd've taken her here.

Bri. . .ach, forget it. He wasn't listening anyway.

This is it, this is the fucking local culture. And what is it? It's shite! LOOK OUT! DANGER! He'd suddenly switched to a shout. The ice is shite! It's cracking up! He waved his hands about in front of him, struggled to get to his feet, but couldn't. It's going to CRACK RIGHT OPEN! You'll all be SWALLOWED RIGHT UP! BEWARE BEWARE! He started laughing, waving his arms at the folk out on the rink. A few of the nearer ones turned to see who was making the racket, though the roaring of the stones and the shouts of the curlers must've covered up most of it.

Shut up, man, I said. It's not going to crack. He had me sweating. I went to stand up, but Bri immediately grabbed my shoulder again in a tight grip, and pulled me down. He put his mouth right up to my ear.

Talking of cracks, he said, Do you want to ken something? Eh? Do you want to, Paddy? Marjorie, right, ken what I call her? Hot Marj! Ken why, eh? Do you ken why? Cause she spreads easy! Get it? Do you get it? Good eh, fucking good! I made that up last night. Well, Dek made it up, that fucking cunt Dek Duguid, he made it up. But fuck him. FUCK HIM! He's no friend of mine. Nuh. He thinks he's fucking smart, slagging the place off, slagging you off, slagging everything off, but. . .he's no friend of mine, that's for fucking sure these days.

He gave a few jerky nods of his head.

But listen, I said, *You* were just newly slagging off the. . .

But *you* are, he said, and gripped my shoulder tighter. You're a real friend, you are. I just want to fucking tell you that, okay? Is that okay? Course it's fucking okay! You and me, we're the same. Not like fucking Dek Duguid, the cunt, not like him. We're mates, eh? Always have been, always fucking will, you cunt. . .

Paddy. It was my granda. Bri fell silent. Would you walk home with me? I'm tired, and the roads are a bitty slippy.

I freed myself from Bri's hug and stood up. Sure thing, Granda.

I straightened my jacket out. Bri, I'm off now. You'll be alright, eh? He didn't answer, just sat there, looking at my granda's knees. Right. Bye then.

Bye bye. Bye bye. Bye bye. He lay back on the frozen grass.

What's all this about the roads being slippy, anyhow? You were skating about on the rink there like nobody's business.

Aye. Well. I just thought you looked like you needed rescued. God save us from our friends! That's what they used to say, that was the old motto.

It's a good one, maybe.

And I *was* starting to get a bittie tired, loon. And cold as well. I feel the cold these days like I never used to. Getting soft!

You're not the only one. God, somebody should get a fire going: set up a brazier at the edge of the rink and let folk stand beside it. No! Rent the space out to them! A pound for five minutes by the fire: roll up!

He chuckled and we walked on. The streets were empty and still, and the only sounds were the faint ones of shouting and cheering and stones roaring and clacking at the curling; and even they faded as we moved away past the dark open space of the pleasure park.

That reminds me, said my granda. There was something I thought of to tell you. About forest fires.

Oh aye. What's that?

Well. You set me thinking about it, ken, and I minded on something after you left last night that would maybe serve for a moral to the story. It's this: after the wind shifted and the blaze went away over the hill towards the breaks at Balfour, well, it did

194

go out. Or so we thought. By the dawning there was nothing to see but a few whisps of smoke coming up from the burnt-out stumps and hulks, and a few red embers and a lot of black ash all over. That's the bugger dealt with, we thought to ourselves. But over the next week or so, new wee fires kept springing up here and there all over the hill. We'd think we'd got them all out, then somebody would spot a new one flaring up and the squad would have to go haring away with the beaters and swat it out. This went on for days, these blazes just jumping up out of nowhere.

So what was it? Bits of smouldering stuff kindling up again?

Aye, well: more than that. It turned out the whole hill was still on fire – under the ground! The peat-layer had got so hot, you see, that it'd caught alight, and now it was smouldering away down there over the whole side of the hill. And every time the peat came across a bit of air – round the roots of a tree or something – it'd burst into life again!

God!

Aye! And I do believe it could've gone on for weeks, if we hadn't had a good downpouring of rain on the Sunday.

That's one good thing about forest fires in Scotland, I said. You can be sure you'll get a good shower of rain pretty soon!

We turned into Albert Street, and walked down the middle of the road. The noise of the curling could no longer be heard. Now there was only our footsteps, and my granda breathing.

But anyway, there you go, loon, he said. You wanted a moral to the story, and there it is.

What? That's not a moral!

It's as close as I get to one.

Hih. I need a moral to the moral, in that case.

He laughed. What is it with you and morals all of a sudden? You shouldn't be worrying about things like that at your age.

I thought for a minute. But when else, Granda? When else?

Is something bothering you? he said after a second.

Well, aye. I have to. . .tell you something. I'm sorry about this, Granda, but: ken that bike of mine, the one my dad used to do deliveries on?

Em. . .

Mind, it has the metal holder for the message basket over the front wheel? It's black. And you used it to do the deliveries on afore my dad, even?

I remember that bike, a terrible heavy old brute. I gave it to young Jamie, and then he lumbered you, did he? So that's what happened to it!

Aye, well, something else's happened now. I lost it.

He stopped. You what?

Well, it kind of got pinched.

Ho!

Well, not exactly pinched. I suppose it was more lost, really. Only. . .well, sorry, Granda. I feel terrible about it.

He looked at me. By heavens, Paddy, you're well shot of that old thing.

What?

He was grinning. I'm sure it was no loss to nobody. And I'll tell you what, you can have my new bike instead. Aye!

Your new one?

Well, I say new. I got it four year ago, I suppose, and it was second-hand then. But it's got gears and everything. Much nippier than that old crate ever was! Aye, come round themorn and I'll've got it out of the shed, given it the once over.

Och no, I can't take it; you need it yourself for getting around, for picking berries and everything. I can't take it.

He shook his head. I'm getting over old for it, Paddy. For all of that.

No! You're not! You're not getting old!

He stopped. We were at the gate of the path down to the Summer House. The big house loomed above us, its windows dark. My granda lifted the latch on the gate, but paused without opening it, and turned to me.

I'd ask you in, he said, But Mary'll maybe be sleeping, and I wouldn't like to wake her up. You still need your sleep when you're old, Paddy, but it's hard to get sometimes.

Ach, that's okay, Granda.

He let the latch fall again and leant back against the gatepost. But afore I go in, loon, we could have a blether here. He looked at me. I mean it's good talking to you loon, you put up with me rambling on. . .

Ach! I shrugged, looked away.

So it's fair enough if you want to ramble on to me for a change. There's something bothering you, Paddy, not just that daft bike, surely. Come on. What's up?

Eh. . .och, I don't ken, Granda. I shrugged again. Well I don't ken how to talk about it. Or if there is anything to talk about.

There's always something to talk about! Come on, tell me.

I frowned. Well, it's more of a question than anything, I suppose — me asking you more stuff as usual! It's about. . .the Kirk Woods. Ken where the old drove road goes through them, right by the Sabbath Stane?

He nodded, looked both ways along the empty street.

Well, eh. . .do you know what I'm going to say, by the way?

He shook his head.

It's just. . . Have you ever seen any strange things going on there, Granda? Or heard about them maybe? Like lights in the wood where there shouldn't be lights? It's been on my mind, this, I can't stop worrying over it. Somebody told me they saw. . .well, have you ever heard of anything there?

Hmm. . .

The thing is, see, once I can work it all out, understand it, then I'll be able to forget about it. It's just cause I don't understand that it's worrying away at me.

He folded his arms, and let his chin sink onto his chest. Well. There is one thing I mind, but I doubt it's just a load of nonsense. Will I tell you?

Aye, anything.

Well, when we were bairns, we used to be great believers in ghosts and spooks and all sorts of things. Or, I'm not sure if we *believed* in them, but we used to tell ourselves stories about them, just to pass the time, or to give ourselves the shivers or something. Anyway, one of these was about a big black horseman that used to gallop along that drove road. He was supposed to turn up at night if you were travelling alone there, and he was supposed to be a big man, wrapped in black, sitting on a big black horse. Some folk said he didn't have a head on his shoulders, but some folk didn't mention that. Which is funny: you'd think it would be the kind of thing you'd notice! Anyway, this mannie wasn't on the go when I was a loon, even – we had the new denside road to use – but folk still talked about him. He was supposed to come charging down on you out of nowhere – especially further down by the ford, not so much up in the woods there – come charging down and send you flying into the bogs at the side of the road. And when you turned to shout after him, as you picked yourself up. . .he'd've disappeared! And you'd be floundering around in the sluch for hours, maybe, trying to find your way out. If you could. . .

After a second I said, That's a good story, Granda.

He sighed. But I reckon that's likely all it is. Though when I was your age, I probably half believed it!

It's hard to know what to believe sometimes.

Probably it was just farmers coming up with an excuse to tell their wives why they were late home. All night in the pub, dear? No! A headless horseman came and ran me off the road! Ho. The only strange lights were the ones at the inn windows!

I laughed at the idea of it, and my granda did too. We both stood there in the still dark street, and shook with laughter.

We'll have to stop this, I said after a while.

Ach, don't worry about the neighbours, they'll never hear us through their double glazing. He looked up at the big house behind him, and started chuckling away again.

No, not that, I said. But I'm in danger of laughing my head off, and then where'll I be? I'll be chasing folk up and down Albert Street from here till forever. Look out, here comes the headless auctioneer's assistant! Yikes!

We laughed some more, and by the time we stopped we were both wiping tears out of our eyes.

I'd better be getting in, said my granda eventually.

Aye. Goodnight then. It's been a good night.

He lifted the latch. And listen, Paddy: mind and come round for that bike, if not themorn then anytime. It's no use to me, but you've the need of it – for your work, or to get to the Auld Mill, or to go out courting even – come and get it, loon!

Running back along Albert Street, the thing that kept going through my mind was the word *courting*, and how it must have something to do with being in court, on trial. And if I was being tried, I was surely failing, surely being found guilty.

I belted through the square. The Auld Mill was in darkness; even Wilson couldn't keep Shona on this late. However late it was. I careered round into the Kinker road, glancing up at the jubilee clock on the hall – twentyfive to one – before running on past it, and the school, and the park wynd, and on and on and on till I came to the last house in the village: Bunce Coban's place, The Rowans.

The house was separated from the road by a slope of yard littered with wrecks of cars, burst engine blocks and piles of tattered tyres. I started picking my way through the junk towards the front door, but there didn't seem to be any clear pathway, and my shins were constantly knocking and scraping against bits of mangled car sticking out of the dark. I was sweating like a horse, my breath coming in shudders, my legs swavery from the running. I wiped the sweat from my forehead, but it kept on coming. It felt like the whole of my body was burning under the skin, somehow, and the fire was boiling my gutful of watery beer into pints of sticky sweat. But at the same time the hard ringing frost of the night was getting hold of my bones, chilling my blood, freezing the air cold enough to jeel my lungs. And the worst of it was, maybe all my running and peching was pointless, maybe I was already too late.

I got up and went on towards the house. The windows were dribbling with condensation, and loud music was bumping out through the glass, mixed with yells and laughter and the thumping of the dancers' feet. I stood on the doorstep for a few seconds, my hand out ready to ring the doorbell, but there was such a hell of a racket going on inside that no one would ever hear it or take any notice. I dropped my hand to the doorknob, pushed open the door, and went in. Bunce's oily overalls and workboots were lying in a heap on the floor of the tiny porch, and various grimy tools lay scattered along the windowsills amongst the shrivelled pot-plants. Through the patterned glass door at the back of the porch, I could see bodies moving about, crossing between the kitchen and the living-room, dancing briefly as they came into the uncrowded space of the hallway. But the light was dim and it was all unclear. I went through the second door.

The first person I saw was Dek Duguid, coming out of the kitchen, a four-pack of cans in his hand. I went to say something, but he walked right on into the living-room without slowing or glancing in my direction. At least I knew where the drink was now, though what I really fancied was a big glass of cool water, and water's not allowed at Blackden parties.

A couple of older women – one of them Bunce's bidie-in, who I'd met last New Year, the only other time I'd been in the house – came out of the kitchen as I went in. They were talking amongst themselves, and didn't notice me trying to apologise for squeezing past them in the doorway.

Hold on to your valuables, it's the auctioneer!

Laughter.

Jock the Cock was sitting at the kitchen table; Joany from the bakers, who'd been one of the pool players in the Mill earlier, was sitting on him. Directly above them the normal lightbulbs had been taken out of their fittings and replaced with red ones. Joany's face was glowing red, her teeth pink, as she laughed at me and shifted on Jock's knee.

Otherwise known as the minister's bum-chum! continued Jock.

Fuck off, I said, but it was drowned out by him and the others laughing again. Wingnut was there, standing in a corner between the table and the window, staring down at the top of his Special Brew can, and Joany's sister, a couple years younger than her, even – fifteen, maybe – she was hanging around too. Plus several other folk I only knew to look at, but who knew me well enough to look at me and fucking snigger. I shrugged at them, and made for the stash of cans and bottles on the worktop by the cooker. I took an export and headed for the door. You missed yourself at the curling, I said as I passed them.

Bollocks, said Jock. Who wants to watch a bunch of old farts getting their hair permed? Joany giggled again, and Jock started bouncing her up and down on his knees. Anyway, he said, I've got all the curls I want, and he jammed his face into the back of Joany's hair and started making roaring noises like a wild beast.

There was somebody in the lavvy, so I looked into the living-room. The music was cranked up full blast and folk were dancing in the middle of the floor. Every so often somebody would bump into somebody else, or trip on the sheepskin rug in front of the log-effect electric fire, and go crashing down onto the big leather settee, which was already occupied by two couples occupied with each other. The air was solid with heat.

Shona was neither dancing nor on the settee nor sitting propped up against the skirting-board smoking and drinking. I was beginning to shit myself that she'd already been and gone and I'd missed her, missed my last chance.

The telly was on in the corner of the room, though the sound was turned down – or just drowned out. Dek was sitting cross-legged in front of it, three full cans at his right hand, ten or so empty ones heaped on his left. As I watched, he lowered another can from his mouth, twisted the top and bottom in opposite directions in his hands, and squashed it flat. He dropped it onto the heap, and immediately picked up a new one. Before opening it, he leant forward to the video, pressed it to rewind, and scrolled the picture back at high speed for a few seconds; then he let it play again, watching the action closely. It was from a kung fu movie, and involved someone being chopped off the top of a high building and landing in the seat of a convertible car passing below, driven by a glamorous woman in a miniskirt. Dek stopped the tape, rewound it to the fight on the rooftop, and watched the sequence from the start.

I tried the lavvy again. This time it was empty, and I went in and locked the door. For a minute I sat on the edge of the bath, trying to get my brain to think clearly, but I kept getting distracted by my reflection in the mirror-tiles opposite. I made an effort not to focus – I'd made that mistake once already tonight –but it was useless: I kept catching glimpses of myself out of the corner of my eye.

I jumped up, went over to the sink, and poured the contents of my can down the plug. Then I ran the hot tap for a second to rinse away any traces of the beer, and the cold one to sluice out and fill up my can.

I'd unlocked the door but not even got out into the hallway when a woman shoved in past me, and there was the sound of retching, and vomit splattering on lino. I pulled the door shut behind me, and stood there, taking a drink of my water. It was slightly tinny tasting, but fine and cool.

Two guys were leaning against the wall to one side of me.

No, it's true, one of them was saying. I fucking read it: he was born at Perth, under a fucking tree or something!

Pontius fucking Pilate?

Aye!

The guy that killed Jesus?

Aye. He was Scottish, a fucking Perther!

Typical Saint Johnstone fan though, eh?

The living-room was even hotter and more crowded than before, but there was still no sign of Shona. It would've been good to know if anyone had seen her leaving – or even if they'd seen her at the party at all. But there was nobody that I knew and that knew her. Except Dek. Shit.

I edged my way round the outside of the room, avoiding the flying feet and elbows, trying not to kick over any of the bottles and cans and ashtrays that were scattered all over the carpet. Dek was still sitting in front of the telly, and the kung fu film was still on the screen, but now the pause button had been pressed, and the picture was frozen – blurred and shivering slightly – just at the point where the guy was falling backwards off the high-rise roof.

I got down on my hunkers beside him. Dek, I said.

He turned his head towards me, but looked confused, as if he was trying to remember something. How to speak, maybe.

Dek, I said. Have you seen Shona anywhere?

Who?

I was beginning to sweat again; I took a swallow of water. Shona Findlay. The chef, ken?

Who. . .are you?

What? It's me, Paddy.

He frowned. What happened to you?

Eh, I was at the curling, and talking to my granda. It was good. You should have a word with him sometime; he worked in the Forestry as well, you ken.

No, what *happened* to you?

For a minute I'd forgotten that we'd fallen out, but now his frown was turning into a scowl, and it was a waste of time talking to him. I stood up to go.

Fuck you, Hunter, he said. Aye, and fuck your granda as well.

I walked off across the room.

Fuck all of you, I heard him shouting over the music. Fuck all of the Hunters!

As I came out into the hallway, Jock the Cock grabbed my shoulder. He pushed me against the doorframe, grinning, breathing rum fumes over my face. Honest, he said, She better watch it, that girl, what's her cunt? The baker's fucking lassie. She's giving me the come-on, and she better watch it. Now I'm just hot, but soon I'll be horny!

She's called. . .

But she doesn't know me, see, she's a young girl, she's never dealt with the likes of me. Ask my wife about it! She'll tell you! But this girl, she takes a drink and she looks at me, she takes a drink and she smiles, she takes a drink and before you know it she's letting me put my hand down her pants. She's fucking asking for it, she's ganting! Fucking up on her hind legs begging!

I drank from my can, looked at him over the rim. Is your wife here, like?

What? No, she's got to stay at home and look after the kids. Four of them we have, you know, beautiful little fuckers. I love them, they're. . .but this is it, see? What this girl doesn't know.

What, that you've got four kids?

No, no. That every time me and Mandy have sex without her cork in, I just blow her fucking uterus out!

What?

Aye, four times in our lives we've had a shag without any protection, and four anklebiters we got out of it. One each time, just like that: pop, pop, pop. Pop. But that's my fucking balls for you, that's the power my fucking balls have!

So are you going to tell her then?

He frowned. Eh, why should I?

You can't go getting Joany pregnant!

No, no, it's not Joany I'm speaking about. It's her sister, fucking gorgeous wee ride! Bit young maybe, but like my dad always said, if they're old enough to bleed, they're old enough to breed!

I turned away and walked as fast as I could towards the front door, jabbed and dunted by dancing and staggering bodies at every step. From the kitchen there was the sound of glass smashing, and a scream, then cheers. I opened the door into the porch, then the main door, and stepped out into the night.

And I closed my eyes and just stood there.

There was a trickling noise. Water emptying from the can as I held it slackly at my side. I brought it up to my lips for a drink. The water tasted warm and stale. I spat out what was left in my mouth, and flung the can as far away from me as I could. It clanged against something in the dark.

What now? I didn't want to go back into the party, but I didn't know what else to do.

I was still trying to decide – or not trying, even, just waiting for a decision to come into my head – when the front door opened behind me, and somebody came out. I didn't turn to see who it was, but after a second I didn't need to.

Aye aye man, said Wingnut.

I opened my eyes.

Time to be heading home, he said.

Is it?

Some folk've got to work themorn's morn.

Eh. . .

No use saying to the beasts when they're drizzening at the hour of the milking, Sorry I'm late, I got stuck at a party.

I suppose not.

When you've got to go, you've got to go! And I guess I'll get going thenow. He started off through the junk.

Wingy, I said after him, Did you see Shona Findlay thenight?

He paused. Eh, aye. She was here till about half an hour ago.

A jolt went through me. Who did she come with?

Nobody that I saw.

Yes! I punched the air.

But she left with Bobby Halcro, going back to his place, I think.

What?

Aye, arms around each other and everything, lovey-dovey stuff. It'd make you sick.

It would that. I looked across the darkness of the yard. Fuck's sake.

Well, like I say, I better be getting to my bed. Are you coming thenow, Paddy? We go the same way, I reckon. Till I turn off at the Shakkin Briggie, anyway.

I started walking towards the road, and Wingnut fell into step beside me.

I'm feeling in a yappy kind of mood, he said. I suppose that's what they call the drink talking! So if you wanted we could. . .

We'd reached the road. I stopped. No, I said. I won't be going your way.

You won't?

No, but thanks anyway, Wingy. I can't talk thenow, everything's too bad. That's how I was looking for Shona, like. Cause she might not be. So I've got to get going. But thanks.

I started walking, heading west, past the Blackden sign and out of the village. I turned and walked backwards for a few steps. Wingnut was watching me go. I raised a hand to wave to him, and opened my mouth to shout something. But I couldn't think what to say, so I shut it and walked on.

Bobby Bastard lived in a caravan about a mile outside the village, not far from my auntie Heather's cottage. Because he worked as a labourer on the estate, the factor had been letting him bide there till he could find a house. It was meant to be a temporary arrangement, but he'd been there nearly three years. From time to time he'd save up a big bundle of money, but would always blow it on drink or dope before finding somewhere permanent to move into.

I turned off the road after fifteen minutes' walking, and headed up the thick rutted mud of the forestry track. It had been driven through the woods to let the log-grabbing lorries in to do their work on the thickly timbered land between the Kinker road and Corse House itself, and I was continually stumbling over the ridges of clay kirned up and the spin-holes dug down by their massive tyres. Against the dark of the trees I could make out the light-coloured track curving away in front, but the starlight wasn't bright enough to show up the detail of what lay before me: the going was rough.

For a long time there was no sign of life at all, and I was beginning to wonder if I'd maybe turned up the wrong track. But just then I started to hear a faint noise – music, voices – and I scanned the trees on each side of the road. Thirty metres ahead, just off to the left, a glisk of light showed through between the treetrunks. I hesitated, then walked on slowly, keeping my footsteps as silent as possible, holding my breath, as I came level with the small clearing and looked in.

The caravan was small and battered. There were no curtains or blinds at the windows, and yellow light spilled out onto a 2CV parked next to it. From inside came the sound of someone strumming chords on a guitar, and two voices – one male, one female – trying to sing harmonies on a familiar-seeming song. I listened, trying to work out what the tune was, but I couldn't, it was too muffled. Something sixties. Bob Dylan, maybe. They started in on another verse, but one of them got the words wrong, and the guitar trailed off with a series of twangs as the two of them broke out giggling. Then the male voice said a few words, a dark shape moved across a window, and the door was thrown open.

I dived back the way from the middle of the track, landed on the long grass of the verge, and rolled over a couple times till I tumbled into the drainage ditch there.

I listened. There were no cries of surprise or fury, no sound of anyone reaching for a torch or a gun, only the man yawning, then saying something in a hoarse voice. There were footsteps, then a faint drizzling noise. Slowly I raised my face from the leaves and mould at the bottom of the ditch; I craned my neck back and sideways, lifting my eyes just above ground-level. For a few seconds I couldn't see anyone, but then I spotted Bobby Bastard at the far edge of the clearing. He had his back to the caravan and was pissing out into the trees, whistling softly.

Before I'd worked out the tune, he'd walked back across the clearing and stopped just in front of the caravan, looking up at the starry circle of sky above him. The door was standing open, and yellow light flickered over his face.

No, it's true, he said. It's meant to be pretty freaky stuff. I mean you get it out of cactuses, so why not tatties?

A female voice said something inside the caravan. It might've been Shona's, or it might not; I couldn't hear it clearly.

This guy was telling me, it's what happened to the Marie

Celeste – ken, that ship where all the crew disappeared. They'd been out at sea over long, and all their tatties had went green and wheeeeee! Hey, captain, the sails are a funny colour! Hey, captain, what kind of a trip *is* this? Hey, captain, let's all go and live with the dolphins! And they all jumped overboard and were never seen again. Great! And they went down in history!

The female voice said something, and Halcro laughed.

Aye, he said. So you make sure I'm nowhere near any water when I try it, or you might never see *me* again!

Would that be a big disaster for me, would it? said the female voice, getting clearer. Would I miss you, like?

Would you not?

Shona appeared in the doorway of the caravan. Her hair was loose over her shoulders, and her shoulders were bare. Maybe she was totally naked, I couldn't see, because Bobby Bastard was standing right in front of her.

I'm not sure, said Shona. Come and show me what I'd be missing.

He stepped forwards, took hold of her, and the door shut behind them as they moved into the depths of the caravan.

For a while I listened for the guitar to start up again, but it didn't. Eventually I was getting a crick in my neck and cramps in my legs, and I raised myself onto my knees and elbows, checked the coast was clear, then stood up.

The candles in the caravan were out, and there were faint noises coming from inside. I couldn't make out what they were exactly. I didn't really want to.

I crossed the track and entered the trees at the side of the clearing. Looking between the trunks, I could get a clear view of the caravan in the starlight; but I'd be completely hidden in the shadows. I watched for a short time, then moved through the trees, searching for the best viewpoint.

Halfway round the clearing, and four or five metres in from it, a big old larch had fallen. It had not quite come to rest on the ground, but had been trapped, its trunk at a shallow angle amongst the dense branches of the other trees around it. The larch's base had been wrenched out of the earth and was sticking straight up, a semicircle of roots and tentacles and fibres, all joined solid with a mass of soil and moss and rotted plant matter. I stood with my back against this wall of roots, my feet in the socket it'd been torn from, staring at the dark windows of the caravan.

I considered marching right up to the door and hammering on it. But Bobby would answer, and he was a psycho bastard. And anyway, what could I say to him? Ever thought of moving into Goodman's bothy to live, Halcro? Much better than here. You could go right now! And oh, leave Shona with me, I want to talk to her. . .

Useless. I'd be severely tenderized for sure.

It was only Shona I wanted to talk to. I'd be better waiting till she came out of the caravan – for a pee maybe – then nipping up to her and taking her down the road a bit and reasoning with her:

Come on, Shona, I want an explanation.

What of?

Everything! Fucking everything! Everything in the world!

And maybe I'd persuade her to leave Halcro for good and come away with me – right there and then, without waking him, even – and the two of us would walk off into the night. And *we* could go to Goodman's bothy, do it up, live there together. . .

Rubbish. It was no good having fucking fantasies about it. This was a time when being realistic and keeping the head screwed on were essential. Fuck's sake, they were always essential! But now more than ever.

I just had to wait till Shona appeared, and take it from there.

I slid my back down the root-wall till I was sitting on the earthy-smelling earth at the base of it. I shivered. The night was cold. I pulled my hands up inside the sleeves of my jacket, and huddled into myself as well as I could.

No sign of life from the caravan. I waited.

Me and Dek and Bri used to be constantly building gang huts and dens when we were kids. It was a favourite thing to do in the summer: build a den all day till you were hot and covered in muck, then bike down the denside and jump in The Dooker to cool off.

We built platforms up trees, and we dug holes in the ground and roofed them with corrugated iron. We made wigwams of branches, with bracken woven in and out for the sides, and we arranged circles of boulders for walls and told ourselves we'd built a castle. Once, after a summer storm had knocked down a tree near to Bri's farm, we built a den up against the roots of it, which were sticking up like the ones I was leaning against now. That was a good den, half the work had already been done for us. We finished it in no time and played in it all weekend. But then Bri's da came and sawed the tree up for firewood, and that den joined the list of all the others that had been wrecked by parents or other kids or gamekeepers or the weather. But we kept on building them. I don't know why. We built them and then, after a

212

day or a week, they got wrecked and we built another one. It couldn't've been the playing in them that was the good bit, that drove us to keep making them, it must've been the building itself. This and the fact that they were our own places, wee houses we'd built with our own hands. They were just how we wanted them to be. They were ours.

I started scrabbling at the earth on each side of me with my hands. I dug my fingers in and scooped them down and pushed the soil and leaf-mould away from me. It was cold and gritty, and it worked its way under my fingernails, but the movement kept me warm at least. After ten minutes or so the tree-socket was a good few centimetres deeper, and I'd built up a small wall of stones and earth round the outside rim of it.

I stepped over the wall and searched the ground about the couped tree. Branches and twigs of all sizes had been torn off by the fall. I picked up some of the right length and propped them at an angle against the root-wall, close enough together that their clumps of needles meshed. Before placing the last branch in position, I got back inside the den, crouched down, and pulled the branch after me, sealing the gap.

I could see out fine between the twigs and the needles; the caravan was in plain view. But no one walking by a couple metres away – let alone stepping out the caravan door – would spot me behind my camouflage. It was the perfect viewpoint. I even had the idea it was slightly warmer than being out in the open under the big night sky.

Resting my back against the root-wall, I gazed across the clearing towards the caravan. Eventually Shona would have to come out, and I'd be waiting for her. And then I'd get things sorted out once and for all.

Sunday

I dreamt I was with my father, deep in the Blackden kirkyard, and woke to find it was true. The dark damp taste of earth filled my mouth, nothing but black was before my eyes, and my bones lay cramped and stiff in a cold bed of worms and pine.

I blinked and the darkness didn't flicker. I ran my tongue round my teeth and tasted earth and decay. I stretched my arms and legs and felt walls all around.

Panic leapt into my brain, I jerked upright – and my forehead banged against something solid and rough, thousands of tiny lashes whipping across my face.

Immediately I remembered where I was and how I'd got there, and why the cold had taken posession of my body. I blinked my eyes again, then turned them to the branched side of my lair. There was no sign of daylight, just a slight thinning of the darkness in the sky, a faint glow of predawn grey about the caravan.

I knew how I'd got here, but not why. Because of Shona? That was what I'd thought. But now that wasn't good enough. It wasn't good enough because she had come back to Halcro's place of her own accord. I had not come to save her or make her see the light. She did not need saved, she saw as much light as I did.

I thought I had come here of my own accord and she had not; really it was the other way round. She had come here freely, while I had been carried away by some black flow of ideas and words and events and just ended up here. When had I first been swept away? A couple days ago? A couple years ago? It didn't matter. All that mattered was that I was about to step out of the flow and go my own way. And the first step out of the flow was the step that would take me out of my den. I was too old for a den. And not old enough for a grave. That was for sure.

I sat up again, wriggled my shoulders and rubbed my hands up and down my legs a few times. Then I reached out, grabbed the nearest branch, and slowly stood up, lifting it clear into the air as I rose. Stiffly, I leant forward and laid the branch down on the ground. Then I stepped out of the den, walked through the trees towards the light streak of the forestry track, and was gone, striding away through the dark woods.

I don't think I even glanced at the caravan as I passed it.

Usually I just walked right in, shouting hello, but now the door was locked. It had a big black iron knocker in the shape of a lion's head. I took it in my hand and chapped it down: once, twice, three times. For a long time nothing happened. Then a movement caught the corner of my eye: a curtain twitching in the window to the right of the door. I turned to face it, smiling, and immediately the curtain jerked back and Heather was looking out at me, a dressing-gown over her shoulders, her hair sticking out in whisps at all angles. She screwed her face up, moved her lips, but I couldn't work out what she was saying, so I just smiled some more and pointed at myself and then at the front door. She mouthed something else, and let the curtain fall shut.

Nothing happened for another long while, then I heard footsteps, a key scraping round in the lock, and a creak as the door opened a little. Heather's eyes appeared in the gap; they switched back and forth.

Are you by yourself? she whispered.

Just me, Heather. My voice was croaky. I cleared my throat. Me on my tod, as per always.

She opened the door a bit wider and stuck her head out, looking left and right and all around the garden. Sorry, she said, But nobody usually comes round this time of night unless it's a certain Calum Roberts, locked out drunk by Tart Smith and looking for sympathy.

No, don't worry, Heather. There's nobody here but me, and I'm not looking for sympathy. And nobody's kicked me out, I just left!

She cast an eye over me. You are drunk though, aren't you, Paddy? Drunk and into a ditch by the looks of you.

I glanced down. Sure enough, my jacket and jeans were half covered in muck and mud, and there were grass stains on my knees and bits of twig and leaf hanging off me here and there.

Hih. I can see why you'd think that, Heather, but no, I'm not drunk. I mean I only had a couple of pints and that was, oh, hours ago. Years ago!

Paddy, do you *ken* what time it is?

Eh, no, no I don't actually. My watch says. . . I pushed back my sleeve and looked at it. Well, my watch has stopped, cause I forgot to wind it afore I went to sleep. Hih! I looked up at the dark sky. About eight, is it?

216

She rolled her eyes. Paddy, it's five to four! In the morning! Oh.

Aye, oh! And I was up till one with the late film and a bottle of wine! Much though I like the pleasure of your company. . .

Christ, I'm sorry, Heather, I had no idea. I took a step back. Well, I reckon I'll hit the road now, I won't disturb you any more.

She opened the door wide and stood back from it. You're going nowhere, she said, pulling her dressing-gown tighter about her. Not after getting me out of my bed in the middle of the night, not when you look like you've been sleeping in a silage pit. You're not just sodding off as if nothing had happened!

Hey, thanks, Heather, I said, and walked past her into the hallway. I could do with a cup of coffee or something: it's freezing out there.

You don't have to tell me, she said, shutting the door and following me down the hallway. Starvation!

Aye, I said, turning into the kitchen. I'm pretty hungry as well.

Ha ha, she said.

The kitchen doubled as her living-room. There was a big square table in the middle of the floor, and a couple of easy chairs; along one wall was a Raeburn stove, with a sink and cupboards at right angles to it; a telly and hifi and books lined built-in shelves all along the third wall. Under the window in the fourth wall was a seat with cushions; I sat down on this, stretched my legs out, and sighed.

Ahhh, it's good to get a rest. And it's fine and warm in here. Magic.

Heather picked up an empty bottle and a red-dregged glass

217

from the table and laid them down on the draining board. Then she filled the kettle and plugged it in.

It's not surprising it's warm, she said. I only banked this thing up two or three hours ago. It'll be going great guns by now.

She sat down on a stool by the stove and opened a wee door in the front of it; a pile of small round coals glowed red and orange inside. Heather took a poker and jabbed it into the fire in a couple of places, and the coals collapsed in on themselves to half their original level.

Ha! Thought so! She laid down the poker. It's good stuff this anthracite, she said, picking up a pair of tongs. It burns for ages. You have to watch it, though. She crashed the tongs into a tin bucket round the side of the stove, and they came out grasping three or four lumps. You have to watch it cause sometimes the separate wee bits of coal get kind of glued together with the heat, kind of welded. You think you've got a real blaze going when really it's just a shell of pieces all stuck together, and underneath the thing's almost dead. All the fuel's gone and nothing's left to burn. So you tap this shell, break it down – even if it looks good itself – so you can see what the real fire's doing underneath. She dropped on a final grip of coals and shut the door, then adjusted a knob just below it. And that's another thing, she said. You have to let some air into it every now and then, especially if you've been piling on new fuel.

Thanks, Heather, I said. All has not been in vain: I've really learned something tonight.

Watch it, or I'll throw you back out in the cold!

I laughed, unzipping my jacket. A blast of heat had come out of the open firedoor, and the temperature was changing from warm to hot. Even my bones were thawing. Over on the other side of the room there was a hottering and a hissing from the kettle, then a click.

218

That's it boiled, I said.

Dear dear! cried Heather, standing up. You're as bad as the rest of them! Stoke the fire, make my coffee, where's my dinner, wash my clothes! She went over to the kettle and started making two cups of coffee.

Sorry, Heather. I didn't mean it like that.

What did your last slave die of?

I've no slaves, Heather.

No, she's escaped to Edinburgh for the weekend, I just remembered!

I jumped up and walked over towards her, hanging my jacket over a chair on the way. Wise up, Heather, me and my mum get on fine: talk of slaves is havers. Maybe my dad treated her like that for the last while, but you ken why that was: he couldn't do things himself.

Och. . . She looked down at the coffee, still swirling round in the mugs after her stirring. I was only kidding.

I don't believe in keeping slaves, and I don't believe in being a slave. I picked up a coffee. Power over no one, and no one having power over me, that's what I want.

Whoo! Watch it, Paddy: you're getting a bit political there! She went over and sat at the table, blinking at me as she passed.

I tried to sip the coffee, but it was still too hot. I sat down opposite her, sliding the mug away for just now. That's what I came to talk to you about, actually: politics.

What? You trauchled all the way out here at four in the morning for a discussion about nationalism? Am I dreaming? I ken it's important, Paddy, but there's a time and a. . .

No, not for a discussion, really. I don't want to discuss it, I just want to tell you: I've been thinking about what you were saying the other night.

Oh aye?

Well, not really thinking about it, but, eh, considering it. Aye, I've definitely been considering it.

I'm glad to hear it. And?

And I thought I better tell you, I definitely won't be coming to any meetings. There's not a chance in hell of me getting involved in your sort of politics.

What? My sort of. . .

It's just I was worried I might've given you the impression that I was kind of interested the other night, that I might well want to get involved. It's been bugging me all weekend. Well, something has, and I think that's a part of it. I wanted to get it off my chest, anyroad, to clear the air I suppose, to clear my head.

Heather reached for a packet of cigarettes and lighter that were balanced on the arm of the easy chair in front of the telly. She lit up, took a draw, looked at me, then breathed out smoke and coughed, a bottom-of-the-lungs job.

Are you alright, Heather?

What! She coughed and laughed. I was just wondering the same about you! Are you feeling alright? I mean, with you being on your own this weekend, have things been on your mind? I mean, too much time for thinking and that. Has it been preying on you?

I looked at her. No. Has what been preying?

Well, you know. . .

I'm always thinking, I said. Not just this weekend. What else is there to do while I'm biking about the countryside, or hosing down the mart or something? The only thing about this past while is I think I'm seeing things clearer than before. It's something to do with the weather, maybe; it's been that sharp and still lately, of course I've been seeing things clearer! It's like God or the devil or somebody has plonked a glass jar down over Blackden and trapped us all – like me and Helen used to do when we were kids, trapping grasshoppers – and he's having a good look at us all, hopping about. But what he doesn't ken is that the glass lets us see the world more clearly too, lets us get a proper fix on it, and when the jar's lifted away we'll all be seeing our way ahead that bit sharper.

She took a sip of coffee and looked at me. Talking of getting ahead, she said, Do you want me to give you a lift home? I mean I don't ken where you've been thenight, but it doesn't look like it was your bed. I could stick on some clothes and we could jump in the Beetle and you'd be home in ten minutes.

Christ, Heather, this is the whole point! I'm fed up of getting lifts here, there and everywhere! Everybody's jumping down my throat to give me lifts every minute of the day. I'm fed up with it, completely scunnered! I want to get somewhere under my own steam for a change!

A long snout of ash had grown on the end of Heather's cigarette. Her eyes moved off me for a second while she tapped the fag over the heaped-up glass ashtray.

Look out! I shouted, jumping up. I grabbed the ashtray from in front of her and stepped over to the stove with it, where I opened the firedoor, flicked my wrist, and sent the pile of butts and ash and a wine-cork flying into the glow and flames. I banged the firedoor shut and tossed the ashtray back onto the table.

There you go, disaster averted! You were just about over-flowing there. One more dowp and the lot would've spilled all over the table. What a mess! But you're okay now, it's sorted, it's nice and empty and clean again and. . .hold on.

I snatched up the ashtray, strode over to the sink, and scooshed a jet of water onto the bits of ash still smeared and stuck to the bottom of it; under the glass was a red and yellow lion-rampant. I shook the thing dry, walked back to the table, and put it down in front of her.

There you are, Heather: as new, as spleet-fucking-new! Oops, sorry about that. But look at it, you could see your face in it, wonderful! Is it not amazing how all trace of the fagarettes just completely vanishes? Maybe you should get a couple ashtrays installed in your lungs, then you could just take them out and rinse them under the tap every few days! Magic!

Paddy, she said, Sit down.

I was up at the far end of the room by the window. I sat on the cushioned seat underneath it, and looked at her.

I'll sit, I said, But I can't stay long, I must get moving on. Listen. . .

My gaze strayed to my leather jacket hanging on the back of its chair. I jumped up, went over to it, and started pulling it on.

Paddy! Will you sit down!

I can't Heather, I don't have time.

You don't have time? It's half-four in the morning, where are you rushing to at this hour?

On, on, I've got to get on.

She caught my wrist as I walked past her. Don't rush off, Paddy, she said. I'm worried about you.

No need!

Look, I'll get a downie out and you can kip on the big chairs for a few hours, get some rest. Then I could give you a. . .hey, I know: I could give you a driving lesson, how about that? You could drive back to The Strath, it's quiet roads all the way! If you're wanting driving lessons, just ask me, Paddy. I passed first time, I did!

It's too late. I pulled away, breaking her grip on my wrist.

Paddy, come and rest for a while, have a sleep, have my bed if you don't fancy the chairs. All I'm saying is, don't rush away.

I'm not rushing, I said. I'm years late already! I did a swerve so she couldn't grab me again, and headed for the door.

She stood up. Listen, Paddy, I can see something's bugging you. Come on and tell me about it. I don't mind just listening. It's good to have someone to talk to.

I know that.

Well then, don't disappear! She stood up. Tell me what's been happening to you, tell me what's bothering you.

Ach. . . I went out into the hallway and Heather came after me. I can't, I said. I'd only burst out greeting or something. It's impossible.

So what's wrong with greeting, she said, following down the hall. Get it off your chest, like you were saying.

I opened the door and stepped outside. No, I said. I can't talk about it now. It's too hard, too much. I started walking away across her lawn.

Okay, not now, she said from the doorway, pulling her dressing-gown tight against the cold again. But if you *ever* want to tell me about it, do, anytime.

I broke into a sprint, leapt over a bed of shrubs at the bottom of the lawn, headed out the gate and onto the track away through the woods. Heather was shouting something behind me, maybe goodbyes, and I opened my mouth to reply. Jets of cold air funnelled down my throat and into my lungs, and my lungs filled and filled up till the pressure was too great to contain, and the air came howling out of my wide open mouth: Whooooooooooo-hooooooooooh!

*

Some time later, I'd stopped running, but was still walking quickly. I wasn't exactly sure where I was going, but I was definitely going. The estate was crisscrossed by a network of tracks and roads and paths, and I followed my nose along one after another of these, hardly noticing where I was heading, never considering whether to turn left or right or go straight ahead at junctions. I just kept going.

I found myself at the end of the Corse Avenue. It stretched out perfectly straight for nearly a mile ahead, and at the end of it were the famous locked and rusted Jacobite gates. I set off towards them.

It wasn't that I wanted to see the gates. I'd been up to them a thousand times before, as had everybody else in Blackden: Up The Avenue was one of the favourite strolls in the area for courting couples, parents with kids, old folk with nothing better to do. But there was nobody out strolling at this hour, and the whole place looked different to me somehow in the three-quarters dark. I strode along, glancing from side to side, trying to work out what it was that was nagging at me. Something about the trees, they weren't looking themselves. They were looking like something else, reminding me of something.

The trees were beeches. They'd been planted a hundred and fifty years before, when half the population worked for the laird, and if he wanted the most impressive garden path on Deeside, then that's exactly what he got. The trees were huge and impressive, but now they were old and grey too, and with their leaves withered and torn off early by the October gales, they were like giant grey bones arching over my head.

That was what had been trying to get into my mind, that picture: me walking through an avenue of bones, the ribcage of some vast creature's skeleton, with the long straight my feet were pacing out the backbone, and the great gaunt trees above me the weather-bleached ribs of the beast. And at the end of the avenue was Corse House – that would be the beast's head – and back where I'd come from, back through the woods beyond Heather's place, there was Blackden: the arse-end of the giant.

I marched on, a shiver going up my own backbone, maybe at the cold of the dawn air, maybe at the thought of where I was walking. For now I was minding on another of my granda's stories, one that I'd heard when I was young and had always remembered. You couldn't forget it if you wanted to, for the proof of the tale's truth was plain to see whenever you raised your eyes to the southern horizon and saw outlined against the sky the black shape of the hill called Clochnaben, with its strange lump and dip side by side on the summit ridge.

The story was this. In the old times, a couple of giants lived on the wooded slopes of the ben, which still had a smooth round top to it, like all its neighbours. But these were not just any old giants, this was the devil and his wife; they'd made the Cloch their home. Now one morning they had a disagreement, and the disagreement led to an argument, the argument led to a row, and the row led to a fight. The next thing folk knew, the earth for miles around was shaking with the stamping of the devils' feet, the air was thundering with the bellow of their voices, and the sun got blocked out as they threw fistfuls of full-grown oaks at each other in rage. The devil-wife had climbed to the top of the ben and was starting to get the upper hand, when the devil – his blood boiling with fury, steam jetting out of his toenails – scooped out an enormous armful of stones and earth and solid rock from the ground by his feet and brought it crashing down on top of her. Then there was silence. Late that afternoon, when the smoke and stew had cleared and the sun was showing its face again, the folk of Blackden stuck their heads out the door, then slowly crept outside and looked south. The shape of Clochnaben was changed forever, with a jagged lump of rock as big as the school on top of the kirk on top of Corse House sticking out of its summit. And beside the rock, his legs dangling in the hole he'd scooped out, sat the devil greeting his black heart out, sorry now for what he'd done in his temper.

And there the story ends, except that if you climb the Cloch to this very day and go right up to the side of the lump on top, you'll see the hole where it came from, and the marks of giant scaly fingers scraped round the inside of the pit. The devil disappeared, it was said, never to return to these parts. When last seen he was heading south.

That was the way my granda told it. But walking along the avenue at the end of a dark night, the beech-bones curving over me like ribs, I was getting the feeling that he'd got the end of the story wrong. The devil *had* come back to these parts. He'd sneaked back some other dark night and laid himself down in the lee of the Braes of Corse, his arse washing in the waters of the Black Burn at the denhead, his head propped up by the big house, gazing across to Clochnaben. And there he'd died, and his flesh had rotted away, till all that was left was his skeleton. And now I was strolling along through the devil's innards, approaching his thrapple's knot. And though the road was dry and solid beneath my feet, it was hard not to see it guttering black and wet with the devil's blood.

I turned off the avenue before reaching the gates, and followed the path worn through the woods there. But instead of taking the usual strollers' loop back towards the village, I headed along a much fainter trail through the trees. I wasn't exactly sure where it went, but I had a rough idea. There were a couple riddles about placenames we had when we were kids. One was, How do you get to Dinnet? Take off the D and you're in it! And the other was, How do you get to the Braes of Corse? Go up the braes and you're there, of course! Well, Dinnet was fifteen miles away up the Dee, I knew I wasn't near there. But I was definitely gaining height.

After a while the trees grew sparser and more stunted, and, after I'd stepped over the tumbled remains of a drystane dyke, they stopped completely and were replaced by heather, whins and broom. The moor rose gently at first and I hardly broke sweat, but after a while the path grew so faint amongst the thick scraggly heather that I lost it in the half-dark. After that the going was harder. The heather dragged at my ankles, twigs of the stuff snagging on my turnups and bootlaces, slowing me down, making me work for every step. I couldn't walk in a normal way now, but had to go in an exaggerated stilting style, lifting each foot high to clear the heather before I could move it forwards and set it down. Soon my knee joints were aching and my muscles burning, but I didn't stop or even pause, just took great gulping breaths and imagined the coolness of the air circulating through my body like smoke breathed into a bottle, hoped that would fool my weary feet into carrying on.

After clearing the treeline, I didn't go straight for the summit of the hill, but took an easier tack round the shallow slope on its west side, so it wasn't till quite a distance further on that I won up to the high ridge and could work out exactly where I was. Behind me stretched the moor in a long series of minor summits and ridges: the Braes of Corse. The heather was dark upon them, with only faint gleams here and there showing where small spring-pools or lochans were catching the last of the starlight, the first of the dawn. There was nothing else except abandoned peat workings and grouse butts till the hills flattened out around Mortlich, ten miles distant.

Ahead was a different story. The line of the hills curved round on my left, cloaked in the Corse Woods I'd just passed through; to my right it ran on and then angled in sharply, dipping down to a low point where the Black Burn and the denside road slipped through it. Framed in the pass was the spiky black shape of Clochnaben on the southern horizon. Directly in front of me, across the den, were the Kirk Woods, with the Sabbath Stane and the old drove road somewhere in their depths; out of the far side of the woods grew the big boot-shaped hill called Ben Macdeamhain, the road to Aberdeen scraping round its lower shoulder. Somewhere in the shadows of its further slope lay The Strath, where I lived, or at least had been living. It seemed like years since I'd been there, and with the sky lightening in the east behind the craggy outline of the Ben, it was impossible to make anything out. For all I could tell, The Strath could've disappeared in the night, swallowed by a big black hole opened under it, leaving no trace of the home I'd always lived in.

At one end of the deep oval glen between the Braes of Corse and Ben Macdeamhain lay the streets and houses of Blackden, half hidden in the trees, half illuminated by yellow streetlamps. At this hour on a Sunday morning, it was very still: no tractors lurching out of parks and courts, no commuter cars speeding off to Aberdeen, no buses dropping off loads of kids at the school gates opposite the hall. But even when all this stuff *was* going on Blackden was still a pretty quiet place, and from up on the hill-ridge where I was sitting – getting my breath back, rubbing my thumbs into the stiff muscles of my legs – it was easy to see why.

The place was completely surrounded by high land. The village looked half-sunk into the earth there at the denhead. Not much wonder the noise of the outside world didn't reach it too often.

Below me and half a mile to my right was a small farm with a straggle of outbuildings and a long narrow track leading down into the trees at the denside. Goodman's Croft! I was back there again! That was the problem with this part of the world, this hollow in the hills: if you didn't watch out you'd spend your whole life whizzing round and round the walls of the den like a motorbiker on a wall of death. Going a hell of a speed, maybe, but never actually getting anywhere. Round and round to the same places, round and round with the same people, round and round with the same thoughts going round and round in your head. I'd only been there eighteen and three-quarter years, and already I was feeling dizzy.

My muscles had eased, my breath was even. I jumped up.

Also available from Mandarin

DUNCAN McLEAN

Bucket of Tongues

'Crisp snapshots of Scotland's seamier side, McLean's short stories happily avoid the pitfalls of sentiment or voyeurism. With titles like "A/deen Soccer Thugs Kill All Visiting Fans", this could be the Scottish Tourist Board's worst nightmare'
The Face

'An urgent new extreme, belching and doubting, reductive, disassociated. McLean wants to capture the unremarkable, but it is his remarkable stories which transport. Expressed here at last is a psychic disorder, so contemporary, so unsafe; here is swaggering, sneering, frustrated, self-scepticism on the pavement'
The Guardian

'. . . his words are picked out of some lingual swill bin . . . as foul and disgusting a diatribe as I have seen in print'
The Herald

'. . . an intelligent new writer, with a sharp and quirky eye'
The Scotsman

A. L. KENNEDY

Looking for the Possible Dance

'This beautiful novel is the story of Margaret and the two men in her life: her father, who brought her up, and Colin, her lover . . . A tender, moving story, punctuated by flashes of comedy and one climactic moment of appalling violence'
Literary Review

'A writer rich in the humanity and warmth that seems at a premium in these bleak times'
Salman Rushdie

'Praise the Lord and pass the orchids – a *real* writer is among us, with a beautiful first novel'
Julie Burchill

'An austere and intense talent . . . A. L. Kennedy turns pointlessness into significance'
Sunday Telegraph

'Here is the most promising of the rich new crop of Scottish writers'
Scotsman

'A novel of undeniable warmth and charm'
Jonathan Coe, *Guardian*

IRVINE WELSH

Trainspotting

'An unremitting powerhouse of a novel that marks the
arrival of a major new talent. *Trainspotting* is a loosely
knotted string of jagged, dislocated tales that lay bare the
hearts of darkness of the junkies, wideboys and psychos who
ride the down escalator of opportunity in the nation's
capital. Loud with laughter in the dark, this novel is the real
McCoy. If you haven't heard of Irvine Welsh before . . .
don't worry, you will'
The Herald

'A page-turner . . . *Trainspotting* gives the lie to any cosy
notions of a classless society'
Independent on Sunday

'The voice of punk, grown up, grown wiser and grown eloquent'
Sunday Times

'A novel perpetually in a starburst of verbal energy – a
vernacular spectacular . . . the stories we hear are retched
from the gullet'
Scotland on Sunday

'Trainspotting marks the capital début of a capital writer.
This marvellous novel might feel like a bad day in Bedlam,
but boy is it exhilarating'
Jeff Torrington

A Selected List of Fiction Available from Minerva

☐	7493 9130 8	**The War of Don Emmanuel's Nether Parts**	Louis de Bernières	£5.99
☐	7493 9962 7	**Senor Vivo and the Coca Lord**	Louis de Bernières	£5.99
☐	7493 9857 4	**The Troublesome Offspring of Cardinal Guzman**		
			Louis de Bernières	£6.99
☐	7493 9720 9	**Man Kills Woman**	D. L. Flusfeder	£6.99
☐	7493 9124 3	**Honour Thy Father**	Lesley Glaister	£4.99
☐	7493 9960 0	**Trick or Treat**	Lesley Glaister	£4.99
☐	7493 9112 X	**Hopeful Monsters**	Nicholas Mosley	£6.99
☐	7493 9819 1	**Lemprière's Dictionary**	Lawrence Norfolk	£6.99
☐	7493 9704 7	**Ulverton**	Adam Thorpe	£5.99
☐	7493 9747 0	**Swing Hammer Swing!**	Jeff Torrington	£5.99
☐	7493 9134 0	**Rebuilding Coventry**	Sue Townsend	£4.99
☐	7493 9151 0	**Boating for Beginners**	Jeanette Winterson	£4.99